STOCK MARKET
CASH TRIGGER

LEARN A SIMPLE TECHNIQUE THAT TELLS YOU WHEN TO GO TO CASH

David Alan Carter

READ THE DISCLAIMER BEFORE PROCEEDING

WITH THIS BOOK

ISBN-13: 978-0-9980210-1-0
ISBN-10: 0-9980210-1-6

Table of Contents

Why I Wrote This Book

You may have heard the expression, "The best way to make money is to not lose it." That's more than just a clever financial bumper sticker. It's a slogan steeped in truth.

While stock market gains magnify stock market gains through the beauty of compounding returns, the reverse has a magnifying effect, too.

An example. Take a $100,000 account and lose 10%, and you're left with $90,000. Or lose 30% and you're left with $70,000. That's straightforward enough. Time to make it up through a market recovery, right? Yes, but look at the gains you'll need just to recover and get the account back up to breakeven. To go from $90,000 back to $100,000 requires an 11.1% positive return, not the 10% that caused the setback in the first place.

And to go from $70,000 back to $100,000 requires a 42.9% positive return, not the 30% that cause the setback in the first place.

In short, the greater the loss, the greater the gain has to be in order to recover the loss. And while investors are fixated with this return and that return, who's beating the S&P and which stocks are hitting all time highs, the ultimate success of any investment plan turns on one simple element: minimizing losses. Let me state that again:

> *The ultimate success of any investment plan turns on one simple element: minimizing losses.*

When I was developing the strategy that eventually became *The 12% Solution*, there was one element that I was determined to include: a mechanism for getting out of risky ETFs and into cash in the event of severe market downturns.

I lived through the Great Recession and like many folks, my portfolio took years to recover. Jump cut one decade, and I'm no spring chicken. A multi-year recovery back to breakeven after some market calamity is no longer an acceptable cost of investing over the long run. I simply don't have the long run. Protection has taken on a larger role in my forays into the stock market.

As a result, *The 12% Solution* had such a protection mechanism built into its DNA. I called it a cash trigger. It's a simplified version of the method I'll be describing in this book.

So why fix what ain't broke? It's true that, within the confines of *The 12% Solution*, that built-in cash trigger works perfectly fine. But that strategy is a tightly-focused model with minimal moving parts. In the broader market of risk-on assets, from the vast array of ETFs to individual stocks, adjustments were necessary.

I have a large portion of my money in *The 12% Solution*, in both traditional and tax-deferred accounts. It automates decision making and lets me sleep at night while delivering returns that beat 99% of money managers. And those funds are protected from another "great" recession by the nature of the strategy.

But I also have a brokerage account where I hold (and trade) individual, high-beta stocks. I can't help myself. I see and I want to buy. And yes, I know they're doing wonderful things in the field of compulsive behavior.

Anyway, it's *that* account that was crying out for protection. This book chronicles my pathway to that protection.

This book is about minimizing losses. Mine, and yours.

Who Should Read This Book

First off, let me state that this book will not appeal to every investor. Nor should it. There will be those investors who have found a way to avoid the need to sell assets and go to cash in order to protect one's portfolio. We'll explore that briefly in the first chapter. (Hint: buy diversified funds and fight the instinct to sell. Ever. It helps to have nerves of steel and a 30-year-plus time horizon.)

There will be those investors for whom selling an asset, whether it's plummeting or not, is at odds with their personal policy to pay no capital gains taxes – long term or otherwise. I get it. One always needs to take into consideration the tax implications of a sale, and those implications will be different for each individual. (Tip: investors can avoid capital gains taxes altogether by selling in tax-deferred and tax-free retirement accounts.)

So who is this book for? Pretty much everyone else. It's for anyone dabbling in individual stocks. It's for fund investors at a point in their lives where large losses can't be tolerated. It's for anyone who believes it would be in their portfolio's best interest to avoid the next Great Recession (2007-2009) when the U.S. stock market lost 57% of its value. Or the dot-com crash (2000-2002), when the Nasdaq Composite lost 78% of its value.

It's for anyone investing in the stock market who wants a tool that will provide a modicum of assurance that losses can be managed. That you're not casting your fate to the wind. That the downside has a limit.

In the coming pages, I'll first ask whether we should be selling at all, ever. Of course, it makes a difference whether we're talking individual stocks or funds. We'll look at one of the more popular metrics for visualizing sell signals, and demonstrate *the very real problem* with that popular metric. And finally, develop a system that protects both stocks and funds against broader-market downturns -- crashes, corrections, and bear markets. *That* is the Stock Market Cash Trigger.

And by the way, the end result will not be some magic formula extracted from supercomputing. We're not doing rocket science here. I didn't invent this system from whole cloth. Rather, it's been more like the gathering up of puzzle pieces that were there on the floor all along. I simply eliminated those that didn't fit, put the pieces that did into a structure, and verified results through backtesting.

For the experienced investor who is knowledgeable in the rationale for selling and familiar with SMAs, you're welcome to jump ahead to the chapter *Building The Stock Market Cash Trigger* and get right to the meat of the strategy. But for new and experienced investors alike who wish to understand the rationale and the thinking that went into the strategy, each subsequent chapter delivers.

Finally, although many readers will be new to the stock market, I don't intend this book to be an intro into stock market investing. For the basics regarding selecting a brokerage firm, setting up a trading account, and executing trades, there are warehouses of books and the Internet at your disposal.

For those new to investing as well as those experienced with its highs and lows, welcome to the *Stock Market Cash Trigger*.

Chapter 1 - Why Sell Stocks?

In a perfect world, we never have to sell. In a perfect world, every investment decision is a good one and our stocks climb higher every day. In a perfect world, there is no jarring "SELL SELL SELL" button on Jim Cramer's desk. No need for it. For that matter, in a perfect world, Old Blue never gets old, I have the same hair now that I had at age 17, and Brussels sprouts taste like chocolate truffles.

Alas, it's not a perfect world. From an investor's point of view, that fact is brought home with the following statistic: in 2016, a total of 99 publicly traded companies filed for bankruptcy protection. Of those, 25 companies had assets greater than $1 billion. And this was in a good year (S&P 500 benchmark up +12% for 2016).

What about a bad year? Well, 2008 (arguably a bad year) saw 136 bankruptcy filings by publicly traded companies, including some big names like Lehman Brothers and Washington Mutual. And 2001, the year of the dot-com crash? That would be 263 bankruptcy filings by publically traded companies. And if you had bought stock in one of these companies and were holding on because that's what you had been told to do from any number of Wall Street gurus? You just lost 100% of your investment.

Beyond total business failings, there are the myriad of companies that lose tremendous value in any given year but still manage to hang on to their public shingles. IBM, for example, lost -43% in the single year 1992. Microsoft dropped -62% in the year 2000. Ford Motor crashed -65% in 2008. Tenet Healthcare took a -51% turn for the worse in 2016. Sears Holdings tumbled -61% in 2017.

Good grief! So...

Why Buy Them In The First Place?

One could make that argument. Stay out of the market altogether. If you had, you most certainly would have avoided Ford's -65% loss in 2008. But, you also would have missed Ford's +336% gain *the very next year*.

Plus, keeping your money out of the market and into something ultra safe, like bank certificates of deposit, will get you maybe 1.1% annually, a full point below the current inflation rate (meaning, you're losing ground every year).

What's the answer?

Well, I'm an advocate for being in the market. Over the long run, real wealth can be yours if you get just a few things right. But I'm not an advocate of owning individual stocks. Boom. There you have it.

> Hypocrisy Alert: I own a *boatload* of individual stocks. And not just any old individual stocks, but largely over-priced, high-beta stocks, the kind that can give an investor the Big Eye at night. So, what's up with that?

What's up with that is I'm human, I have frailties, and I sometimes buy an individual stock because I get it in my head that I'm a genius stock picker who can mop the floor with those pinheads on Wall Street. You can probably guess what's wrong with this picture.

All fun aside, here's the problem with stocks: each pick requires research; you're not adequately diversified unless you own dozens across multiple asset classes; and one misjudgment can wipe out months, if not years, of returns.

If you don't *have* to buy individual stocks, avoid them and buy ETFs or mutual funds instead. And in particular, buy those funds that track indices (and are not actively managed with stock pickers of their own to muck up the returns). Even one or two carefully selected ETFs will keep you diversified, reduce the risk inherent in individual stocks, and make selling (if/when you have to) less onerous.

But if you can't help yourself, and *do* own individual stocks, you need to know the...

Warning Signs That It's Time To Sell

I should stipulate that these are warning signs that it's time to sell a stock *based on the company's actions* (or lack thereof), as opposed to any macro-economic trend in the offing. This is just a little extra burden the stock picker bears that the ETF investor can largely ignore.

For starters, understand that there is no magic wand. The data that feeds a decision to sell is fluid; it requires judgment, and that judgment is part art and part science. But there are a few things that most analysts will agree are red flags. Let's look at them briefly. And keep in mind that the following red flags apply to individual stocks (we'll address funds a little later).

RED FLAG #1 – THE COMPANY'S COMPETITIVE ADVANTAGE IS DIMINISHING

A company's competitive advantage can be anything from low prices (i.e. Walmart) to patents (i.e. IBM and Apple), to branding and marketplace goodwill (Coca-Cola). And it's that competitive advantage that provides a moat of protection around the company, keeping at bay would-be competitors.

But if those competitors can build a better mousetrap or find a better way of serving customers, that competitive advantage can disappear quickly. Walmart is currently in a pitched battle with Amazon with the latter having introduced the convenience of online shopping to competitively low pricing. And behemoth IBM has long been losing market share to more nimble competitors that have been able to adapt more quickly to changes in, among other things, the personal computing marketplace -- with a long, slow slide in share price reflective of that loss.

With most companies, holding some form and degree of competitive advantage is a key ingredient in future growth. Diminish that advantage, and future growth – and the company's corresponding stock price – is suddenly in jeopardy. Be prepared to sell.

RED FLAG #2 – CHANGES IN LEADERSHIP

Some companies are built on the visionary leadership of their founder. Think Apple and Steve Jobs, Microsoft and Bill Gates, and Facebook and Mark Zuckerberg. What happens when those companies lose their visionary leader?

While dramatic changes in leadership can dramatically alter a company's future performance, it doesn't have to. An engineering mindset, lofty goals, and a unique corporate culture can be so imbedded in the company that existing employees or fresh management can take the reins and drive performance to the next level. But visionary founders bring something to the table that others often lack. Whether it's the product or service instincts that put their company on the map in the first place, or a star quality that attracts positive media and investor attention, loss of a company founder often marks a turning point.

When Bill Gates turned over the reins of Microsoft to Steve Ballmer in 2000, the company entered a 13-year period of missed opportunities and botched product introductions. And a share price that lost 35% of its value. Conversely, when current CEO Satya Nadella took over in 2014, Nadella promptly imbued the company with a new personality, got some important things right (like cloud computing) and investors have witnessed a more than doubling of Microsoft's stock to date.

Change is unavoidable, and most successful companies will end up losing their formidable founders at some point. That doesn't have to be a death sentence. But if you're holding the company's stock, the event needs to get your attention. Is the business model that made the company successful up to this point still intact? Evaluate the new leadership; do you feel they can pick up and carry on? Or does uncertainty cloud the company's future. If the latter, be prepared to sell.

RED FLAG #3 – SALES ARE FLAGGING

Sales are a key driver of company growth, and companies that deliver revenues that increase at a faster rate than competitors are considered growth companies – and often deliver share prices that outperform as well.

But sales don't go straight up forever. The overall economy, for example, can take a toll on sales of even the most aggressive companies. But the economy aside, a trend of declining revenues can signal problems. It may be a first sign that the previous competitive advantage is diminishing. Or it could be that the product or service is reaching a saturation point in the marketplace.

The once innovative concept of the smartphone has become so ubiquitous that it's now more aptly labeled a commodity, like light bulbs and salt. And with that market shift comes shrinking revenues as key players that were once engines of growth fight for scraps among a shrinking customer base.

Whatever the reason, stalling or falling sales spell trouble for a company's share price. Absent a corporate history of acquisitions, or an imminent campaign to drive new technologies or products to the marketplace, flagging sales may signal a sell.

RED FLAG 4 – EARNINGS ARE SHRINKING

Among all the metrics employed by legions of analysts to predict the future, quarterly corporate earnings are probably the most scrutinized. Earnings are simply the after-tax net income of a company (the revenue left after deducting expenses, interest, and taxes).

Shrinking corporate earnings is a red flag. While there can be some good reasons for a decline in net profit for a particular period of time, (a company redirecting a larger share of revenues to research and development, for example, or a marketing push to drive a new product), a trend of shrinking earnings absent such qualifiers can be signaling that the company is having trouble managing costs. Or having trouble meeting revenue goals without throwing money about wildly.

If you're beginning to see a trend of shrinking quarterly corporate earnings without a corresponding surge in responsible investments, be prepared to sell.

RED FLAG #5 – A DIVIDEND CUT

Not every company pays a dividend. Those that do are often prized by investors seeking marketplace maturity and a stable income. And those companies that raise their quarterly dividend payments are often signaling optimism about the future, garnering even more goodwill from investors.

Conversely, companies that cut dividend payments, regardless of the spin placed on the action by management, are often signaling tough times ahead. Dividends are usually paid out from company earnings. If a company sees earnings weakening in the future, dividends are one of the first things on the chopping block.

Of course that's not always the case: freeing up cash by reducing dividend payouts could be used for R&D, factory expansion, or some other arguably useful purpose. But any cut in dividends should send up a red flag. Unless it's crystal clear the cash that would have been dividends will now be spent in support of growth, be prepared to sell.

WHAT ELSE?

There are, of course, other reasons that you might want to sell a stock. There may be personal reasons that you need to raise cash. Understandably, priorities change, and every household is subject to the occasional financial crisis. Of course, that's a good reason to begin planning now for such eventualities, including keeping a rainy day fund separate from your investment/retirement accounts so you won't be forced to sell equities that you would rather hold.

Speaking of being forced to sell equities at a time not of your choosing, that would fit the description of the margin call. Extend the reach of your (hoped for) stock gains by borrowing from your broker (margin), and be prepared to have to sell those stocks at the worst possible time if they – or the general market – turn against you.

Avoid that scenario by avoiding margin.

Chapter 2 - Why Sell ETFs and Mutual Funds?

If you've decided, for whatever reason (they're all good) to invest through ETFs and mutual funds -- especially those funds that mirror major indices -- the next question becomes: is there ever a case to be made for selling *these*?

The Case For Never Selling

Dalbar, Inc. is the nation's leading financial services market research firm. One of the industry components they measure is investor behavior. Over a recent 30-year period, the annualized rate of return for the average investor in an equity mutual fund has been +3.66%. That, according to the latest 2016 release of Dalbar's Quantitative Analysis of Investor Behavior (QAIB).

To give that some perspective, the U.S. inflation rate for the same period of time was an annualized 2.65% per year. Meaning, for the 30 years ending December 31, 2015, the average equities mutual fund investor was getting ahead by a paltry 1% a year.

It gets worse for investors trying to protect themselves from downside risk by spreading their investments among equity and bond ETFs. Over the same 30-year period, the annualized rate of return for the average investor in a blend of equities and fixed-income mutual funds has been just 1.65%. Factor in inflation, and those investors have actually lost ground.

What makes this so troubling is that the S&P 500 index produced an average annual return of +10.35% during that 30-year period. But that's not what investors got, even investors who bought the funds that mirrored the S&P 500.

What's wrong with this picture? Why such a gap (of almost 7 percentage points) between the returns of actual fund investors and the returns that could be expected from holding representative indices? According to Dalbar, there are a number of factors including: the periodic need for cash (planned and unplanned), fund expenses (i.e. management fees), and voluntary investor behavior.

The latter is by far the largest contributor to investor underperformance. So what is this *bad* investor behavior that so drives down investment returns? Three things: panic selling, excessively exuberant buying, and attempts at market timing.

You might call this Investor Psychology 101. Investors (you, me, professional money managers) are constantly tempted to chase returns. With the chase on, excessively exuberant buying drives up prices beyond the rationale of the company fundamentals. Before long, we're looking at a correction waiting for a catalyst.

When a fund or stock begins going down in price, the average investor can handle it for a while. But if that downward action is accompanied by increasingly negative economic news, political turmoil, or any of the other known catalysts of crashes, the odds are there will come a point when the pain of the paper loss crosses a threshold and becomes too much. The investor hits the sell button. This is panic selling. The fear, of course, is that the fund will continue to plummet and drag your portfolio down to the center of the earth.

Sadly, the average investor typically reaches that pain threshold at or near the bottom of the trough. The behavior is so predictable they've got a name for it: capitulation. It's the kind of panic selling that builds momentum, exacerbates volatility, floods the market with securities that are being sold at lower and lower prices causing yet more selling. It all spirals down dramatically toward a cyclical bottom.

But the average investor doesn't know the bottom is in sight and doesn't understand that psychology. Getting out at any cost becomes paramount because he sees no bottom.

> *There is one thing all market corrections have in common: they eventually stop correcting.*

But there is one thing all market corrections have in common: they eventually stop correcting. And now begins the second of the two-part humiliation: the average fund investor, burned and spooked by a market correction, is now reluctant to get back in.

With individual stocks, there may be good reasons to get out and stay out. But with the market as a whole, and funds that reflect that market (or some portion thereof), every correction has been followed by rally back to breakeven and then up from there. That rally may be head-spinningly quick or long and hesitant to fulfill. But the average fund investor, spooked and burned, will miss some or all of that recovery.

Multiply that behavior a few times? Welcome to the 1.6% average annual return.

Now admittedly, +1.65% annually (or +3.66% for equity-only fund investors) is better than nothing. Holding cash during that time would have generated nothing, putting cash holders at an even greater disadvantage to the ravages of inflation.

But 1.65%? Really?

Really.

One obvious solution is to buy those equity funds, or that mix of equity and fixed-asset funds, and hold on for dear life. And I do mean dear life. Shrug at marketplace euphoria knowing a correction is around the corner. And steel yourself during those inevitable crashes.

Statistically, a market correction of -10% will happen once a year on average. Every couple of years, you can expect a -15% correction. And every 3.5 years: -20% or more. Recognize that market corrections are a healthy part of a normal marketplace expansion. It helps knowing that after a drop of -10% to -20%, it typically takes just 4 months for the market to get back to breakeven. Bear markets (greater than -20%) require longer, 2.7 years on average by some estimates.

By never selling (in a panic or otherwise), the buy-and-hold crowd never miss the boat once market corrections and crashes begin their recoveries.

Buy and hold, and if you have a 30-year-plus time frame, you should come close to matching the indices your funds are mirroring, less management fees. In the grand scheme of things, those are pretty good returns.

If I lose you now, I'll understand. No need to keep reading. After all, an 8% to 10% average annual return is awfully hard to beat. And easy to achieve! Just buy the market, hold what you buy, ignore the periodic sound of train wrecks.

Best of luck, and it's been nice having you as a reader.

The Case For Selling

What? Are you still here? I thought--

OK, if the argument for buy-and-hold didn't take, I can only think of 4 reasons an investor might be prompted to sell the likes of ETFs and mutual funds.

1) You bought the wrong fund.

2) You need to raise cash.

3) You don't have a 30-year time horizon for holding investments. A 5 or 10-year horizon, for example, makes buy-and-hold considerably more dicey. If that's the case, it makes perfect sense not to want to follow a crashing economy down into the depths of a recession knowing your portfolio may not have time to recover before you'll need that money.

4) You want to make more than the 8% market average afforded the buy-and-holders who can wait for the payout.

This book can't help you with 1 and 2. But 3 and 4? Well, we'll see what we can do.

***

Earlier, we touched on a set of red flags that might signal to an investor it's time to sell an individual stock, signals that have nothing to do with macro-market trends. And of course, there may be a reason or two to want/need to sell an ETF or mutual fund.

But assuming we're happy with our fund selections, or happy with our stock picks (no red flags), how do we go about protecting those assets in the event of overall market downturns?

That, of course, is the crux of this book.

On a side note, there are whole training courses devoted to hedging one's trades with the likes of swaps and derivatives, but such "insurance" can be complicated, can get expensive, and effectiveness can be elusive. And because of that, beyond the scope of this book.

For investors holding stocks, mutual funds, or ETFs who are looking to protect those assets simply and effectively from market crashes and the like, we're going to focus on a more elementary solution.

That would be GETTING THE HELL OUT OF DODGE. Preferably, before being carried out of Dodge in a pine box. Translation: selling those risk assets in times of peril and moving into cash.

If that sounds an awful lot like trying to time the market, yes, we're talking about trying to time the market. The same dreaded market timing that makes up one-third of the trifecta of voluntary investor behaviors that consistently shaves almost 7 percentage points off average annual returns.

What? Are we crazy?

> *Market timing is the act of moving in and out of the market or switching between asset classes based on predictive methods such as technical indicators or economic data. --Investopedia*

Admittedly, the idea of market timing has gotten a bad reputation -- and deservedly so. Numerous studies (including those by Dalbar) confirm that the vast majority of actively managed portfolios that move in and out of the market underperform those that are passively managed.

But why? Two reasons: 1) it's really hard to predict the market, and 2) the average investor is constantly embroiled in a pitched battle with fear and greed. Yes, there are some technical indicators that can foreshadow potential calamitous events. But even for the investors who understand those technical indicators, there is a difference between watching them unfold on a paper chart and acting on them in a live trading scenario.

An all-too-common example. A stock or fund you're holding begins slipping and finally hits some technical indicator on a chart, and you dutifully sell because that's what you do when you're a technician following a timing scheme like a simple moving average (we'll be seeing more of this in a moment). Boom, sold.

But then, no sooner than you've sold, sentiment changes; the stock or fund reverses course and starts heading back up. Panic sets in! People you don't know know something you don't know! And you're about to miss the boat! So you buy back the stock/fund, only at a higher price than you had sold moments (or days/weeks) ago.

Whew, that was a close call. You didn't lose too much money, you rationalize, and now you stand to gain what people you don't know are about to gain. And then, guess what? The stock/fund makes another u-turn and proceeds back down. Realizing that your first call was the correct call, you sell once again, this time exacerbating your losses.

Whew, that was a close call. Maybe now is the time to move away from the computer screen and-- wait! What's that thing doing? It's going back up? What the--

You can imagine what happens next.

It pains me to admit, but that was me in any number of trades throughout the years. It might seem comical, but I suspect at least some of you can relate. The point is, I know how hard it is to implement a timing strategy. Even without the clownish back and forth on the buy/sell button, many investors fool themselves into thinking they are perfectly rational investors when in fact they are slaves to the gods of fear and greed.

So, how do we make market timing work? And make it work with individual stocks as well as ETFs? How do we turn a loser's game into a winner's game?

Here's how. We're going to take emotion and guesswork out of the equation and replace it with a cold mechanical strategy. And then we're going to test that strategy to demonstrate that it works.

Chapter 3 - Popular Technical Indicators For Selling

Let's digress for a moment and recall that discussion about red flags, warning signs that it's time to consider selling an individual stock. Well, here's the trouble with red flags: you've got to do some work to root them out, then evaluate the degree to which those red flags portend a future now in question. And on any given day, week, quarter, you'll likely find competing flags, some red, some green, and some polka dot (OK, maybe not polka dot, but certainly every shade of gray).

Then you've got your ETFs and mutual funds which are, in effect, baskets of individual stocks. Because of diversification, each individual holding weighs less on the overall basket. But these funds can and do trend down at times from the weight of their underperforming components -- most notably those funds that mirror narrow sectors of the market.

What is a Simple Moving Average?

You say you don't have time to devote half your day every day to researching your stock and fund picks? I hear that. But what if you could take all the pretty flags – red, green and otherwise -- fighting for attention in quarterly earnings and annual reports, company press releases, and the daily machinations of analysts, TV commentators and assorted gurus, and organize them into some sort of visual structure? Say, perhaps, lines on a chart?

And while we're fantasizing, why not imagine that those lines on a chart could tell you when to buy, when to hold, and when to sell? Further, what if you could glean those buy and sell decisions in a minute or two of gazing vs. hours of toil over financial pages?

It's no fantasy. It's a moving average.

A moving average is a visual representation of the average price of a security over a period of time.

A moving average (MA) is simply a series of past data points plotted on a chart. In the case of a simple moving average (SMA), those data points are calculated by taking the arithmetic mean of the closing prices of an asset for the past X number of periods.

For example, to calculate a basic 10-day SMA for a stock or ETF, you would start by adding up the closing prices for the past 10 days and divide by 10. That result is a data point. Put it on a chart. The next day, repeat the process and come up with a second data point. Put it on the chart in a timeline after the first. Do the same for data point #3, #4 and so on. Connect the data points and you've got a moving average line.

It's that resulting line that's valuable to technical traders, and can help us determine trends -- whether driven by macro events or conditions specific to the individual security. And (maybe?) buy and sell signals for a given security or ETF.

We'll see about that last part.

One thing's for certain: that moving average line beats researching red flags all day and night. Why? Because each data point is a price (an average price, to be accurate) and prices in general reflect all the news and analyses surrounding securities, as well as speculations and ruminations regarding future news.

At least that's the theory behind market efficiency and the efficient market hypothesis (EMH). Formulated by Nobel Laureate Eugene Fama half a century ago, the theory suggests that at any given time, the price on any particular stock -- or the market in general -- fully reflects all available information.

While there is a cottage industry built up around arguing the finer points of that theory, suffice it to say that one look at a stock's price action the day after an earnings announcement speaks volumes. You may have poured over the financial numbers the night before, identified a red flag or two, or seen nothing but green. In the end, it matters little compared to the market's reaction the morning after and in the coming days. And those market reactions turn into dots on the line.

Of course, there may be an overreaction to the numbers, either to the upside or the downside, an overreaction that will retrace to a mean over time. Market efficiency doesn't mean that every investor acts with steely cold efficiency. There's panic selling and over-exuberant buying in every corner of the market in every second of the day. That helps explain why some people (i.e. Warren Buffett and the rare day trader) can outperform over the long run.

But for the most part, and certainly for our purposes in deciding whether or not to sell a security or a fund, a series of price points identifying a trend is valuable stuff.

So, how do we identify a trend with price points? Well, even without an SMA, a line of data points representing closing prices will drift upward or downward over time, often spurred on by catalysts like earnings reports that come in above or below expectations. The direction of that drift is the trend.

The addition of a moving average line on the chart simply improves visibility. It provides a baseline with which to compare price performance, and makes changes in the trend more obvious. In that perfect world we referenced earlier, the two lines (the data points representing closing prices, and an SMA) will tend to run parallel. In our imperfect word, there will be times the two lines will intersect, or cross. For many investors, those crosses identify buy or sell triggers.

Sidebar: We're about to look at the first of many charts and tables in the book. For those unfamiliar with touchscreen tablets or e-readers, you can often enlarge the image in one of two ways.

1) Double tap the image. You can sometimes double tap it again for further enlargement, and to move the image about your screen with a finger.

2) Long press on the image to highlight it. Once highlighted, several options will appear above the image -- including a magnifying glass. Press that magnifying glass to enlarge the image.

Regardless of the method used, to return to the normal page, tap the X in the upper right corner. Physically rotating the tablet or reader to landscape position will also enlarge long charts and graphics.

Let's look at a 1-year chart of Apple showing the 10-day, 50-day and 200-day simple moving averages.

Figure 1

Apple Inc. (AAPL), 2017

Chart courtesy of Barchart.com

In Figure 1, notice that the 10-day SMA (the solid GREEN line) follows the jagged price line much more closely than the other two. The 50-day (the solid BLUE line) curves more gently, and is intersected by the price line a couple of times during the year. The 200-day SMA (the solid RED line) isn't breached by prices at all in the 12 months -- even in the face of two short-term selloffs that swung the 10-day line down dramatically, the 200-day SMA didn't budge.

So, the longer the time frame, the greater the lag in following prices. Our 10-day moving average, for example, will cling to prices quite closely and turn soon after prices turn. On the other end of the spectrum, the 200-day moving average takes its sweet time in moving in the direction of prices. After all, it's dragging around a boatload of data points (200 to be exact). And into that boatload, each subsequent price point matters less than it would in a 10-day SMA. So changes in pricing, even severe price drops or severe price pops, require further, sustained price action to begin moving the longer SMAs.

Popular SMAs and Why The Time Frame Matters

In theory, there are an infinite number of simple moving averages one might construct, limited only by the number of time periods one wishes to use in the calculation. In practice, there are really only a few that matter. Yes, you could march to the beat of your own drum and pick some oddball SMA like a 43-day, but because the rest of the investing community ignores that time frame, its value is questionable and results would need to bear out in testing.

On the other hand, commonly used SMAs, like the 50-day or the 200-day, lay bare important clues that drive investor behavior. To look at it another way, as a stock's price approaches the widely-observed 50-day SMA (for example), it becomes an object of increasing focus from the investor community. And the stock's reaction after intersecting that SMA will foretell its future *to a very slight degree*. Now, *a very slight degree* might sound like nothing, but in the world of investing, a very slight degree is an advantage.

So, we'll confine ourselves to commonly employed SMAs in considering their value in the buy/sell decision process.

Why does a price line crossing an SMA indicate a sell for many investors? Because when the day-to-day closing prices of a security has slipped below the moving average line, it indicates investor sentiment has turned negative – *with respect to the time frame indicated in the SMA*. For that time frame, there are simply more sellers than buyers, and those sellers each day are willing to accept a lower and lower price just to get out.

For those new to investing, keep in mind that it's always a tug of war. For every seller looking to get out for fear the stock is only going down further, there is a buyer willing to step up, believing the stock will rise. Trends can and often do stop on a dime, turn and reverse themselves. But as time goes on and there is no reversal, a momentum develops that increases the likelihood that the trend continues and makes it harder for a reversal to gain traction.

The price line crossing a 5 or 10-day SMA is significant mostly to short-term traders. Ten days is heavily influenced by marketplace noise, which is fickle and can reverse quickly. In short, ten days does not a trend make.

On the other hand, by the time a price line crosses a 100-day or a 200-day SMA, much of the marketplace noise has been filtered out and an actual trend is starting to emerge. For much of the investing community, once that cross is made on a long-duration SMA, an inflection point has been reached. Blow through it and stay through it for a few days, and the stock is either in a confirmed downtrend or a confirmed uptrend (depending on the direction).

But Here's The Trouble With SMAs

Let's go back and look at the performance of Apple during the year 2017. The investor who had bought and held Apple would have seen a +48.5% return for that year. Spectacular. The investor who was working the 50-day moving average, selling when the stock dipped below that average and buying it back when it crossed back above, would have made 8 trades for the year (4 sells and 4 buys). Assuming that investor was holding cash while he was out of the stock, his return for the year was +33.6%. Still spectacular by most measures, but he left +14.9% of his money on the table -- not counting trading commissions and the potential for capital gains taxes if trading in a traditional brokerage account.

Note: in this hypothetical matchup, the investor working the 50-day moving average was placing trades *on the day of the cross*, a distinction that will come into play in a moment.

Over a longer term? Let's go all the way back to the year 2000 so we can catch the dot-com crash. From 2000 to 2017 (17 years), the buy-and-hold Apple investor saw a significantly higher return than the investor working the 50-day moving average.

- Buy-and-hold = 5,042% total return
- 50-day SMA = 1,692% total return

Now don't get me wrong: either of these two returns are so far above the average as to be in nosebleed territory. But for the investor thinking he could *improve* on Apple returns by employing a 50-day moving average, that strategy failed dramatically.

Before we go any further, let's examine a little more closely the day that trades are made. In our example, our investor was placing buy/sell trades on the day of the cross (the day the stock's price line crosses the moving average line). That would seem the obvious time to place such trades.

The problem is, that generates a lot of trades because not every trend reversal sticks. There's an awful lot of testing of the moving averages by investors; breaking through and then retracing, going back at it again in a few days, and retracing. A trend may indeed reverse (they all do eventually), but the event will often play out in fits and starts. And each fit and start costs the investor in time (glued to the computer day in and day out) and money (trading commissions).

For the sake of argument, let's suppose our investor placed his trades just one day a month -- more specifically, the last trading day of the month. And that he would base his trading on whether or not the moving average was above or below the stock's price line *on that day*. No watching the charts daily or even hourly. In fact, ignoring the stock completely until the end of each month.

One thing is certain: his trades on Apple would have been dramatically reduced, from hundreds down to dozens. But what about returns?

Well, with Apple, he wouldn't fare so well. He'd go from +1,692% down to +1,120% in total returns over the 17 years. So, does that settle it? Should we decide the fate of the argument based on one stock?

Let's look at a few others.

-- Amazon: +235% vs. +936.1%. End of month wins.

-- Exxon: -41.0% vs. +82.1%. End of month wins.

-- Home Depot: +85.1% vs. +65.5%. Day of cross wins.

-- Intel: +68.4% vs. +11.7%. Day of cross wins.

-- IBM: +59.4% vs. +66.0%. End of month wins.

At this point, I'm going to call an audible and switch the way we approach trading the moving averages -- from day of cross, to end of month. From these few samples and others, there appears to be a slight advantage to trading end of month. Not every security accommodates. But that slight advantage, coupled with dramatically fewer trades and less time in front of the computer cinches the deal for me.

Let's get back to Apple, but with end-of-the-month trading in place. And this time, let's try the 200-day moving average. In 2017 (Figure 1), we can see that the price never dipped below that line, so both of our hypothetical investors would have remained fully invested, each gaining +48.5% for the year.

Over 17 years? It looks like the buy-and-hold Apple investor wins again, though by a lesser degree.

- Buy-and-hold = 5,042% total return
- 200-day SMA = 2,570% total return

[Note: in the SMA strategy, money was either invested in Apple or in a Vanguard money market fund, a proxy for cash.]

Now, it could be argued that Apple is a unique case among U.S. corporations. Perhaps it's an anomaly. How might the SMA strategy hold up with different securities (and

ETFs)? Let's put Apple together with 9 other widely-held securities, as well as 3 popular ETFs, in Figure 2 (below).

Remember, the following numbers are 17-year total returns unless otherwise noted, comparing buy-and-hold investing vs. a strategy of buying and selling based on the position of the 200-day simple moving average of the individual security at the end of the month.

Figure 2
Buy & Hold vs. Trading the 200-Day SMA (2000-2017)

Security or ETF...	Buy & Hold	200-Day SMA	+ / -
Amazon (AMZN)	1,436.2%	2,002.1%	+565.9%
Apple (AAPL)	5,042.3%	2,570.3%	-2,472.0%
Exxon (XOM)	222.0%	126.3%	-95.7%
Home Depot (HD)	289.3%	393.1%	+103.8%
Intel (INTC)	65.8%	102.5%	+36.7%
Intl. Bus. Machines (IBM)	93.7%	24.1%	-69.6%
Microsoft (MSFT)*	490.9%	69.6%	-421.3%
Pfizer (PFE)	103.5%	112.2%	+8.7%
Wal-Mart Stores (WMT)	97.1%	12.4%	-84.7%
Wells Fargo (WFC)	388.1%	72.2%	-315.9%
S&P 500 (SPY)	154.6%	395.8%	+241.2%
Nasdaq 100 (QQQ)	91.0%	215.2%	+124.2%
Russell 2000 (IWM)**	291.1%	241.2%	-49.9%

* Backtest from December 29, 2000
** Backtest from December 30, 2001

In looking over these returns, the first question I had for myself was, why the heck didn't I buy Apple Computer, Inc. back in 2000?

The second question was, how are we supposed to build a strategy from this data? It's all over the map. Some stocks and ETFs benefited from a 200-day SMA strategy, others went down in flames. If this sampling was any indication (and I picked them without knowing how they would behave), you're rolling the dice as to whether or not you would benefit from such a strategy if applied to some particular stock or ETF you were holding.

OK, so it appears that end-of-the-month buying/selling the 200-day moving average of an individual security is no better than rolling the dice. In the strategy's defense, max drawdown was almost always reduced versus a buy-and-hold plan. So was volatility. Even so, if you're holding the wrong stock or ETF, you could pay a very high price for those benefits.

This might be a good time to mention that trend-indicating strategies *in general* are not return enhancing (although they can be for some stocks and funds). Rather, their primary appeal is in their ability to reduce risk. Which the 200-day SMA achieves through reduced drawdown and volatility. Small comfort, I know.

What About The Golden Cross and Death Cross?

Traders and the financial commentariat frequently refer to "crosses" made when two moving averages intersect on a chart. Most notably, crosses between the 50-day and the 200-day moving averages.

When the 50-day moving average rises above the 200-day moving average, it's called a "golden cross" and is considered a bullish sign. When the 50-day moving average crosses below the 200-day moving average, it's called a "death cross" and considered a bearish sign. See Figure 3 for an example of the latter (day-of-cross trading).

Figure 3

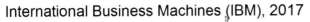

Chart courtesy of Barchart.com

Traders are known to stalk charts waiting for a cross of these two SMAs, and trade accordingly. But do the results actually support this strategy?

Let's punch the numbers. In Figure 4, as before, these are 17-year total returns, unless otherwise noted (the years 2000-2017).

In this case, we're comparing buy-and-hold investing vs. a strategy of trading the security based on the position of its 50-day SMA relative to its 200-day SMA (buying when the 50-day is above, and selling when the 50-day is below).

End-of-month trading.

Figure 4

Buy & Hold vs. Trading the 50/200-Day SMA Crossover (2000-2017)

Security or ETF...	Buy & Hold	50/200-Day Cross	+ / -
Amazon (AMZN)	1,436.2%	2,157.3%	+721.1%
Apple (AAPL)	5,042.3%	3,463.5%	-1,578.8%
Exxon (XOM)	222.0%	90.1%	-131.9%
Home Depot (HD)	289.3%	164.5%	-124.8%
Intel (INTC)	65.8%	181.1%	+115.3%
Intl. Bus. Machines (IBM)	93.7%	-18.3%	-112.0%
Microsoft (MSFT)*	490.9%	18.5%	-472.4%
Pfizer (PFE)	103.5%	70.9%	-32.6%
Wal-Mart Stores (WMT)	97.1%	12.0%	-85.1%
Wells Fargo (WFC)	388.1%	155.5%	-232.6%
S&P 500 (SPY)	154.6%	302.0%	+147.4%
Nasdaq 100 (QQQ)	91.0%	444.3%	+353.3%
Russell 2000 (IWM)**	291.1%	154.0%	-137.1%

* Backtest from December 29, 2000

** Backtest from December 30, 2001

Yes, there were a few successes among these examples. But take a look at IBM, the subject of our "death cross" example in Figure 3. Playing this strategy, you not only would have missed a 93.7% gain at the end of 17 years (modest by any measure), but you would have actually lost money.

Well, that was a bust. Like the 200-day SMA strategy before it, playing the crosses is pretty much a gamble. No telling whether your stock or fund will come out in the green or the red until a sufficient period of time has passed. And given a sufficient period of time, we're all dead.

At this point, a reminder is in order. Let's highlight it in a sidebar.

> Sidebar: Trend indicators are not, in general, return enhancing. They can be, but where they often shine is in their ability to reduce volatility and drawdown. They are primarily protective measures. And in that sense, moving averages may have a role to play. So why this book's focus on enhancing returns? Don't we care about protection? Actually, we care deeply about protection. But we kinda like returns, too. We're driven to have our cake and eat it, too.

The takeaways from these exercises? If I had to hazard a guess, I would say that SMA trading strategies fail to predictably and consistently beat buy-and-hold because there are a lot of head fakes and false signals in the marketplace, times when a security or fund appears to be moving in one direction only to end up reversing course and moving in the other. We alluded to this earlier.

This is especially true for individual stocks; they move to the beat of their own drums in addition to taking marching orders from the overall market. And speaking of the overall market, the broader the index and the larger the cap rate of stocks that make up that index, the fewer the false signals. Hence, the more consistent outperformance when applying either of these strategies to SPY and QQQ.

In addition, the days of largest gains (and losses) for individual stocks tend to cluster. Miss a few days of above-average gains, and you lose out on the compounding effect (generating earnings from previous earnings) of those gains for years to come. The SMA strategies we've outlined do not appear particularly good at capturing those gains.

Whatever the reasons, if we want to have our cake and eat it, too, we need a different approach.

Chapter 4 - Building The Cash Trigger

In looking back over the 17 years of data reflected in the previous tables, one thing stood out to me -- while individual stocks prices are largely driven by their own dynamics (i.e. earnings, management, competition, etc.), there is no mistaking the fact that stocks are influenced by macro economics.

In 2002, at the crux of the dot-com crash, semiconductor chip maker Intel plummeted -50.3%. Of course, being a tech stock, that makes a certain kind of sense. But consider retailing lion Home Depot. In the same year, the company saw its stock price plummet by -53.1%.

And the years 2007-2009? In the throes of the Great Recession, there were no safe havens among equities; high cap, small cap, growth, value, dividend payers, utilities -- everything equity got sucked into the vortex.

In a more normal downturn, as if there is such a thing, there are often pockets of equities that are hit less hard than others. Still, it's tough to get excited when your utility stocks only plunge -20% compared to a broad market crash of -25 or -30%.

The elephant in the room in all of this is not an elephant at all. It's a bear. Macro-level bear markets are what we're trying to avoid. Yes, we'd certainly like to be out of individual stocks and funds when they decide to take a dip, whatever the catalyst. But the one thing they all have in common is their susceptibility to macro-level bear markets.

So let's address the macro for a moment.

In considering a different approach from the moving average of individual stocks and funds, and coincidently laying the foundation for the Stock Market Cash Trigger, let's first note a pattern of investing quite familiar to frequent traders: risk-on risk-off. This catchy phrase simply reflects the observation that investment activity is driven by changes in investor risk tolerance.

Risk-On, Risk-Off

When risk is perceived as low, investors tend to buy higher-risk investments with the lure of higher returns. This low-risk perception in the marketplace leads to "risk-on" behavior on the part of investors.

What causes investors to perceive market risk as low? Positive corporate earnings leading to analyst upgrades. Favorable macroeconomic data. Accommodative central bank policies that encourage economic development. A stable political environment. And other factors. As investors feel the market is being supported by strong fundamentals, they perceive less risk and are more willing to invest for speculative growth and high yield.

Conversely, when risk is perceived as high, investors tend to unwind their stake in risky assets and gravitate toward lower-risk investments that offer more protection for their principal (the original amount of their investment, sans any earnings or accrued interest). This high-risk perception in the marketplace leads to "risk-off" behavior.

What causes investors to perceive market risk as high? Corporate earnings collectively coming in below expectations and leading to analyst downgrades. Contracting or slowing macroeconomic data. Uncertain central bank policy. Politics in turmoil. And other factors.

Why does it matter?

It matters because a move en masse into risk assets (assets that have a significant degree of price volatility, such as equities, commodities, currencies, and real estate) tends to drive up the prices of those assets. At the same time, it drives down the price of safer investments such as U.S. Treasury bonds, gold, and other safe havens, as these are the assets investors are unloading in order to pile into stocks and such.

Conversely, a move en masse into safe havens (e.g. bonds and gold) will drive those associated prices up, while driving down the price of stocks as investors run for the exits.

It matters *to us* because the risk-on, risk-off pattern of market behavior, with its associated influence on asset prices, might just give us our strategic timing.

What is a Market Regime?

As we note from the previous section, investors are generally either chasing returns or chasing safe havens depending upon market risk assessments at any given time. When that market risk assessment takes on a broad consensus, we might call that a regime.

> *Regime = a basic financial relationship that governs asset prices for a period of time.*

At the risk of oversimplifying the myriad dynamics at play in the financial markets, I'm going to funnel us toward the notion that there are but two regimes, risk-on and risk-off, between which the market jumps back and forth. Yes, I know that there are 50 shades of gray between risk-on and risk-off. But sometimes, simplicity works. By the end of this book, see if you don't agree.

So for our purposes, these two regimes are the opposite sides of a coin. Both sides broadly provide the motivational underpinning that governs the actions of the financial markets for a period of time. But those market actions are quite different depending on which side of the coin is up and in command.

And depending upon which market state, or regime, is up and in command, we intend to either make money -- or protect ourselves from losing it.

Determining which of the two market states is in play at a given time is the next step.

Identifying The Current Stock Market Regime

At times it's easy to see which regime the market is in. When stocks are hitting new highs day after day, when market commentary is largely positive, when new money is flowing into equities, it's pretty obvious that we're in a risk-on regime. But when that sentiment begins to sour and stock prices come under pressure, it becomes harder to make that call.

Get out too soon, and you risk standing on the sidelines with your cash while the market turns on a dime and roars to new highs. Get out too late, and you've ridden the coaster down into the trough.

At what point does the market timing investor know for certain that a regime switch as occurred or is about to occur?

Perhaps the most popular technical indicator for just that is the 200-day moving average. Money managers, hedge fund titans, television talking heads and gurus of every degree of repute use the 200-day average to help them gauge market sentiment. Specifically, they look to see whether the market – the S&P 500 in particular – is positioned above or below that indicator line. Above, and the market is in a risk-on regime. Below, and we're in a risk-off regime.

But wait-- we've seen the trouble with moving averages. As we demonstrated in Chapter 3, using moving averages (and MA crosses) of individual stocks and funds to identify entry and exit points will leave you guessing whether you'll have more or less money over the long term than employing a simple buy-and-hold strategy.

But let's go back to the 200-day moving average as applied to the ETF SPY. If we look at our recent tables, SPY actually did outperform quite well when using the 200-day SMA strategy (and the "cross" strategy, for that matter). And SPY is the ETF that mirrors the performance of the S&P 500 index, the most widely cited gauge of large-cap U.S. equities.

What if, instead of looking at the specific SMA of every individual stock or fund we own to determine individual entry and exit points, we generalized. And by generalize, I mean what if we used the SMA from a single asset (SPY) to determine entry and exit points for every security and fund on our list. While that sounds dangerous at first blush, let's see how it plays out.

We've already done the calculation for SPY (see Figure 2). The difference is, now we're going to take each of the other stocks and funds on our list and determine the returns after applying the 200-day SMA of SPY.

In other words, if SPY is trending above its 200-day moving average at the end of the month, we assume a "risk-on" market environment and we buy the security or fund in question (MSFT, IBM, XOM, and the others). If SPY is trending below its 200-day SMA, we assume a "risk-off" market environment and we sell the security or fund in question.

We're going to ignore the SMA of the individual stock or fund, and instead base our buy/sell decisions on the SMA of SPY.

Here we go.

Figure 5

Buy & Hold vs. Trade on 200-Day SMA of SPY (2000-2017)

Security or ETF...	Buy & Hold	Trade on 200-Day SMA of SPY	+ / -
Amazon (AMZN)	1,436.2%	2,393.8%	+957.6%
Apple (AAPL)	5,042.3%	8,843.5%	+3.801.2%
Exxon (XOM)	222.0%	253.6%	+31.6%
Home Depot (HD)	289.3%	429.6%	+140.3%
Intel (INTC)	65.8%	468.3%	+402.5%
Intl. Bus. Machines (IBM)	93.7%	78.2%	-15.5%
Microsoft (MSFT)*	490.9%	519.6%	+28.7%
Pfizer (PFE)	103.5%	226.7%	+123.2%
Wal-Mart Stores (WMT)	97.1%	26.3%	-70.8%
Wells Fargo (WFC)	388.1%	498.0%	+109.9%
S&P 500 (SPY)	154.6%	395.8%	+241.2%
Nasdaq 100 (QQQ)	91.0%	579.0%	+488.0%
Russell 2000 (IWM)**	291.1%	540.1%	+249.0%

* Backtest from December 29, 2000

** Backtest from December 30, 2001

As you can see by Figure 5, basing our buy/sell decisions on whether SPY is trending above or below its 200-day simple moving average has dramatically whittled down the red on the table.

Regime-O-Meter

So, have we found our Regime-O-Meter? A test that will tell us whether we're in a "risk-on" or a "risk-off" market environment? I believe we have.

> *Regime-O-Meter = the position of SPY's price line relative to the ETF's 200-day simple moving average when observed on the last trading day of the month.*

Looking at a chart incorporating SPY's 200-day simple moving average, if SPY's price line is trending above that average on the last date on the chart (the right side of the chart), the market regime is "risk-on." If the price line is below the average, the market regime is "risk-off."

> <u>Sidebar</u>: As I mentioned early on, there's no rocket science involved here. Nor are we inventing something that will shock the cigars out of the mouths of Wall Street barons in their leather chairs. The idea of using the 200-day SMA of the S&P 500 index as a barometer of market health is nothing new. We are, however, tinkering with the usual context and setting up the barometer as a once-a-month instrument. And then we're applying that tool to all manner of securities and putting it to the test. And more importantly, we're not done yet.

We see now how to determine if the broader market is in a "risk-on" or a "risk-off" sentiment. And we've also learned that some market downturns, such as the Great Recession, sucked down all risk assets indiscriminately. Given these two premises, it would seem logical to conclude that a regime change from risk-on to risk-off *is* the Cash Trigger. Meaning, buy and hold risk equities or funds during "risk-on" regimes, and sell those equities or funds during "risk-off" regimes.

So, are we done here? Do we have our Stock Market Cash Trigger?

For some, maybe. But at the risk of opening up a tangential opportunity/can of worms, let me try a simple tweak to the most recent table.

If you'll remember, when the strategy is underway and SPY crosses below its 200-day simple moving average, we sell the risk asset and go to cash. Up until now, we've used the Vanguard money market mutual fund VMFXX as a proxy for cash. It's about as flat a return as you can get, year in and year out, short of stashing dollars under the mattress (an average annual return of 0.37% over the past 10 years). But more importantly, we picked this fund because of its long history -- it facilitated our backtesting to the year 2000.

There is, however, an ETF that has gained in popularity since its inception in July, 2002. That would be SHY, the short-term (1-3 year maturity) Treasury Bond ETF from iShares. Given the trading benefits of an ETF, and the high marks this fund receives from both the analysts and investors, not to mention a slightly higher annual return, let's see what happens if we plug this fund into our formula.

Figure 6 (below) shows total returns of our sample stocks and ETFs when VMFXX is employed as cash throughout the 17-year duration, versus having SHY take its place as the cash proxy from 07/31/2002 to the end of 2017.

Note: the +/- column this time refers only to the difference in total returns of using SHY as our proxy for cash from 07/31/2002 on.

Figure 6

Comparing VMFXX *Alone* versus VMFXX *Plus* SHY (2000-2017)

Security or ETF...	Trade 200-Day SMA of SPY (VMFXX)	Trade 200-Day SMA of SPY (VMFXX & SHY)	+ / -
Amazon (AMZN)	2,393.8%	2,592.2%	+198.4%
Apple (AAPL)	8,843.5%	9,555.2%	+711.7%
Exxon (XOM)	253.6%	281.8%	+28.2%
Home Depot (HD)	429.6%	471.8%	+42.2%
Intel (INTC)	468.3%	513.5%	+45.2%
Intl. Bus. Machines (IBM)	78.2%	92.4%	+14.2%
Microsoft (MSFT)*	519.6%	568.9%	+49.3%
Pfizer (PFE)	226.7%	252.7%	+26.0%
Wal-Mart Stores (WMT)	26.3%	36.3%	+10.0%
Wells Fargo (WFC)	498.0%	545.6%	+47.6%
S&P 500 (SPY)	395.7%	435.2%	+39.5%
Nasdaq 100 (QQQ)	578.9%	633.0%	+54.1%
Russell 2000 (IWM)**	540.1%	591.0%	+50.9%

* Backtest from December 29, 2000
** Backtest from December 30, 2001

Well, I think it's safe to say that the addition of SHY trounced VMFXX alone. If we were to sum up the Cash Trigger strategy at this point, it would look like this: The Stock Market Cash Trigger is...

What? Wait! Did you see what just happened?

When our stock market Regime-O-Meter told us to go to cash, we initially bought the Vanguard money market mutual fund VMFXX. That was fine and dandy, but then we swapped out SHY for the money market fund beginning in 2002, and saw returns edge up, in some cases considerably (i.e., 711 percentage points when trading Apple).

So, what was that difference again between those two funds? VMFXX is made up primarily of U.S. government agency obligations with average maturities of 60 days or less. SHY is made up primarily of U.S. Treasuries with average maturities of 1-3 years.

So, the opening up of the tangential opportunity/can of worms goes like this: what would happen if, instead of investing in cash or cash proxies during market downturns, we invested in even longer-term bonds or Treasuries? Or better yet, what if we could devise a mechanism for determining which, among a number of bond options, would offer the best results?

What we're imagining is something similar to sector rotation. Most often associated with areas of the economy in which businesses share similar product or service, (i.e. semiconductor manufacturers or consumer services companies), there's no reason the concept of rotation can't be applied to the fixed-income market.

In short, the idea is that whatever sector (or bond fund?) has outperformed recently should continue to outperform for a period of time (the essence of momentum investing, confirmed by decades of data). When that time is up, another sector/bond fund that had been out of favor will rise in the ranks to become the outperformer. The investor rotates from one to the next, catching a bit of that outperformance.

In our case, once our Regime-O-Meter tells us the market has entered a "risk-off" environment, perhaps long-term Treasuries are poised to outperform other bond funds for a period of time. In that case, we would want to be in them. On the other hand, maybe whatever is impacting the equity market is also taking a toll on long-term Treasuries, and a different bond fund (or cash proxy) is the way to go.

In fleshing out this bond rotation idea, let's first identify the bond funds we're going to be rotating among.

First up, TLT, the iShares ETF that tracks a market-weighted index of bonds issued by the U.S. Treasury with remaining maturities of 20 years or more (inception date: July 22, 2002). Why? Because it has a frequent negative correlation to equities (making it an effective hedge), and because long-maturity Treasuries have price swings that most closely approximate the price swings of the overall stock market.

But a "frequent" negative correlation doesn't mean it *always* reacts in the opposite direction of the stock market. A number of factors can and do influence long-term U.S. Treasuries, and those influences sometimes drive the bonds in the same direction as stocks for extended periods. When this happens, these Treasuries lose their hedge.

And if the direction is down, losses in equities are matched by losses in long-term Treasuries.

So let's look at additional bond funds that perhaps behave differently to marketplace stimuli than TLT while still providing an equity hedge.

At first glance, selecting ETF alternatives beyond TLT appears daunting. One online database of ETFs (ETFdb.com) puts the number of bond ETFs at over 300 and counting. There are ETFs relating to municipal bonds, corporate bonds, emerging market bonds, government bonds (domestic and international), high-yield bonds, inflation-protected bonds, preferred stock/convertible bonds, and bonds that sample the total bond market.

But a lot of these bond ETFs duplicate one another. And most of the others are fairly easy to determine whether or not they fit our criteria: that they contribute to a rotational strategy that improves CAGR, or lowers volatility, or reduces max drawdown, or some combination of the three.

While my research and testing was by no means exhaustive, two ETFs kept popping up that fit the above criteria.

-- JNK, the SPDR Bloomberg Barclays High Yield Bond ETF that tracks a market-weighted index of highly liquid, high-yield, U.S. corporate bonds. Inception date: November 28, 2007.

-- MUB, the iShares National Muni Bond ETF that tracks an index of investment-grade U.S. municipal bonds. Inception date: September 7, 2007.

These two ETFs, coupled with TLT and VMFXX, will comprise our bond rotation universe. (Note: while SHY beat VMFXX when the two went head-to-head, in combination with the other rotation alternatives, the Vanguard money market fund won out.)

<u>Bond Rotation Universe</u>:

> JNK
> MUB
> TLT
> VMFXX

Now the challenge becomes identifying which of the 4 candidates is demonstrating the most strength relative to the others. That is, which of the 4 funds is outperforming at a given point. In a "risk-off" regime, that's the one we'll buy, under the assumption outperformance begets outperformance – at least for a period of time.

Relative Strength

If you're an experienced trader, you've likely run across a technical analysis tool called the Relative Strength Index (RSI). While useful in its own right, the way I'm going to approach relative strength *is not the same as the RSI.*

Note: we are NOT going to be using the RSI.

Here's the critical difference: The RSI measures the average number of "up" closes vs. the average number of "down" closes over a period of time -- for a single security. In other words, it measures the historical closing prices *for one and only one security.* With RSI, there is no comparison among securities.

In this book, when I talk about relative strength, I'm referring to which asset among multiple assets is strong relative to the others. The key is... among multiple assets.

For our purposes, relative strength is the determination that a security or fund is performing strong relative to another (or relative to multiple others).

So, now that we've defined relative strength for our purposes, why is it important? Because securities or funds that show strength relative to others tend to do so for a period of time. Conversely, securities or funds that show relative weakness to others tend to do so for a period of time. This has been borne out by numerous studies over the years, and is broadly generalized as momentum.

An increase in the price of a security, in and of itself, should not necessarily lead to further increases. The fact that it does is a market anomaly, and to explain such would require us to delve into the realm of behavioral economics and cognitive biases.

We're not going to do that; we're going to accept that momentum is real. And we're going to go about taking advantage of it.

In finance, momentum is the empirically observed tendency for rising asset prices to rise further, and falling prices to keep falling. -- Wikipedia

Let's see relative strength in action. Figure 7 shows two industry peers, Honeywell (**RED** trend line) and 3M (**BLUE** trend line) plotted on the same chart for a period of 3 months ending December 29, 2017.

Figure 7

Relative Strength: Honeywell vs. 3M

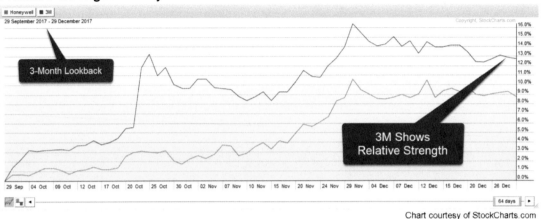

Chart courtesy of StockCharts.com

One glance clearly shows 3M outperforming Honeywell over 3 months, demonstrating relative strength in this matchup.

Another example, this time with the municipal bond fund MUB (**RED** trend line) and the long-maturing Treasuries fund TLT (**BLUE** trend line).

Figure 8

Relative Strength: MUB vs. TLT

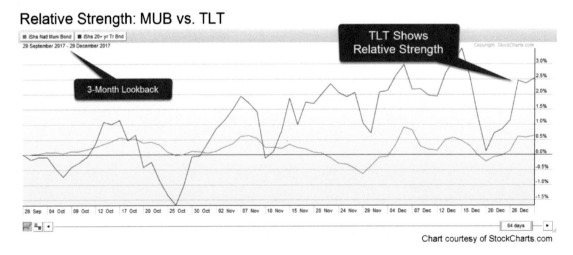

Chart courtesy of StockCharts.com

So that's what it looks like. But there is one huge variable at play: the time frame.

Determining outperformance requires a time frame in which to judge performance. Call that the "lookback" period. If we line up a few stocks or ETFs and *look back* over a day, we can clearly see which stock or ETF outperformed its peers *for that day*. Same with a week, a month or six months – we see outperformance for that week, that month or that 6-month period.

But relative performance based on a lookback of a single day or even a week is not particularly useful to us.

Markets -- including the fixed-income markets -- fluctuate constantly. In trying to price thousands of assets in real time, markets (i.e., investors) succumb to all manner of trending news, crisis headlines, word-of-mouth rumors, the prognostications of analysts and talking heads, program trading, and the deliberate manipulations of professional traders to manufacture market advantages.

It's largely noise and has no lasting impact on value, yet that constant noise is constantly affecting asset prices in the short run.

> *Noise = stock market activity caused by trending news, rumors, program trading, dividend payments, or other phenomenon that is not indicative of overall market sentiment.*

In general, the shorter the time frame, the more difficult it is to separate meaningful market information from noise. Putting some distance on noise - in the form of time - allows the truly important information to rise to the top and begin to have a more relevant impact on asset pricing.

But too much time can render a relative strength test ineffective, as well, by diluting the importance of meaningful information that is beginning to drive a momentum shift.

Pick too short a time frame and noise-driven price fluctuations rule. Pick too long a time frame, and top-performing assets become less predictable for the upcoming month.

So what's the Goldilocks lookback – a time frame that's not too hot, not too cold?

Crunching the numbers with our data partner ETFreplay.com, a 3-month lookback (that's 63 trading days) appears to be optimal -- when comparing two or more equities or funds to determine a short-term (month or two) momentum play.

So, if I was a stock picker determined to buy one or the other of our industrial giants going into January of 2018, I'd give the nod to 3M as the stock more likely to outperform in the coming month or so due to the market anomaly of momentum.

Similarly, if I was going to choose either MUB or TLT for the upcoming month, I'd give the nod to TLT as it is showing relative strength going into the month.

A 3-month lookback, coincidently, also happens to be darn convenient, as most stock charts have a preassigned 3-month button on their interval lineup.

Putting Relative Strength To The Test

Now, I've made some pretty bold claims with respect to relative strength, momentum, and the notion that outperforming assets will continue to outperform for a period of time.

Let's take a moment to make sure that works.

We've got our time frames: a monthly rotation schedule during "risk-off" regimes, and a 3-month lookback period to determine the relative outperformer for the upcoming month. With such a rotation scheme, the bare minimum objective should be to show improved results over simply buying and holding any one of the individual bond funds that make up the scheme. Otherwise, just buy and hold that one fund during "risk-off" times.

From 2008 to 2017...

-- If you bought and held JNK, your total return would have been 70.90%.

-- If you bought and held MUB, your total return would have been 46.40%.

-- If you bought and held TLT, your total return would have been 87.90%.

-- If you bought and held VMFXX, your total return would have been 4.10%.

-- If you <u>rotated among the 4</u>, your total return would have been 209.40%.

Well, that seems to work. As an added bonus, rotating averaged out the volatility and max drawdown inherent in holding any of the 4 funds separately; for example reducing TLT's volatility of 15% to a more reasonable average of 12%.

OK -- let's perform this (hopefully) last experiment on our budding Cash Trigger strategy. In lieu of a fixed investment in cash or a cash proxy during "risk-off" regimes, we're now going to invest in one of the 4 bond funds from our universe, selected by using the relative strength test outlined above.

Keep in mind that each successive month during a market downturn could mean a different bond fund selected. So, trades will likely increase.

Here we go. Again, 17 years of backtesting (the first two and a half years limited to the money market fund).

Figure 9

Buy & Hold vs. Trade on 200-Day SMA of SPY *with Bond Rotation* (2000-2017)

Security or ETF...	Buy & Hold	Trade on 200-Day SMA of SPY (Bond Rotation)	+ / -
Amazon (AMZN)	1,436.2%	4,124.8%	+2,688.6%
Apple (AAPL)	5,042.3%	15,051.6%	+10,009.3%
Exxon (XOM)	222.0%	499.1%	+277.1%
Home Depot (HD)	289.3%	797.3%	+508.0%
Intel (INTC)	65.8%	862.8%	+797.0%
Intl. Bus. Machines (IBM)	93.7%	202.0%	+108.3%
Microsoft (MSFT)*	490.9%	949.7%	+458.8%
Pfizer (PFE)	103.5%	453.6%	+350.1%
Wal-Mart Stores (WMT)	97.1%	113.9%	+16.8%
Wells Fargo (WFC)	388.1%	913.1%	+525.0%
S&P 500 (SPY)	154.6%	739.9%	+585.3%
Nasdaq 100 (QQQ)	91.0%	1,050.2%	+959.2%
Russell 2000 (IWM)**	291.1%	984.4%	+693.3%

* Backtest from December 29, 2000

** Backtest from December 30, 2001

OK, that heading for Figure 9 is a mouthful, but here's what that means. With each of these individual stocks and ETFs, on the last trading day of the month, we looked at the 200-day simple moving average of SPY in deciding whether to own them or not. If we did *not* own them, we owned one of four bond funds decided by a relative strength test.

And the results, as compared to a buy & hold strategy (the first column of numbers) is nothing short of amazing. We've pretty much gone from a sea of red (in the beginning, trading each individual security to its own 200-day SMA) to a sea of green. I think we've got it.

So, The Cash Trigger Is?

The Stock Market Cash Trigger is a mechanical system for 1) identifying a switch in the broader market regime, from an environment of "risk-on" to "risk-off," and for 2) managing the aftermath of that switch.

Identifying The Market Regime

We determine that such a switch has occurred by employing our Regime-O-Meter. That is, once a month, ideally on the last trading day of the month, we pull up a stock chart of SPY (representing the benchmark S&P 500 index) and its 200-day simple moving average.

If the price line for SPY is trending above its SMA line on the last date on the chart (the right side of the chart), the market regime is "risk-on." If the price line is trending below the SMA line, the market regime is "risk-off."

Managing The Aftermath

-- In "risk-on" regimes, we hold our selected risk assets, be they equities or funds.

-- In "risk-off" regimes, we sell those risk assets and...

1) hold cash (or buy and hold a cash proxy like SHY), or
2) buy and hold one of 4 bond funds determined via a relative strength test.

Wash, rinse, and repeat.

Selecting A Bond Fund

In "risk-off" regimes, as noted above, we have the option to buy and hold one of the 4 preselected bond funds (ETFs) from our bond universe. This option will maximize our returns over the long term. Here's what we do:

On the last trading day of the month, after determining that the broader market is in a "risk-off" environment, we will chart the relative performance of these 4 ETFs to determine which one is showing relative strength going into the next month. The ETFs for our consideration are as follows: JNK, MUB, TLT, VMFXX.

We gauge relative performance by using a stock chart that provides for simultaneously comparing multiple stocks or ETFs – either the stock chart that is incorporated on the Web pages of your brokerage account, or one that is readily available through both paid and free Web services. For illustration purposes throughout this book, I've used free charts constructed from StockCharts.com (specifically, their "PerfCharts").

Once the ticker symbols of the 4 ETFs are entered into the chart, and a 3-month time frame selected (the lookback period), the ETF with the most relative strength will become evident: it's the one whose graph line is uppermost on the chart as of today's date. That's the ETF we will buy to hold for the following month until the process repeats on the last day of the following month.

Note Regarding VMFXX

Not every stock chart will have the mutual fund VMFXX in its database. If it doesn't, not to worry. VMFXX is about as close to cash as you can get, which also means it's about as close to the "zero" line on a stock chart as you can get. If your chart provider doesn't have the fund, just plug in the remaining 3 bond ETFs.

Should all 3 of those ETFs end up trending below that zero line, that's your cue to either go with VMFXX , or -- to make life easy -- simply hold your cash in your broker's money market fund (which is usually automatic whenever you sell a security).

Chapter 5 - A Year In The Life

Let's take one year in the life of the Cash Trigger, and see how the mechanics of the system would work on a month-by-month basis. I'll pick 2010, because I know the trigger will kick in during that year.

For this example, we'll be putting Home Depot to the test. But remember, it doesn't matter the risk equity or fund. We're not evaluating them, per se. Rather, we're deciding whether or not to hold *any* risk asset based on the relationship between SPY and its 200-day simple moving average.

So, the first stop in our Cash Trigger strategy is to have a look at SPY and its 200-day SMA on December 31, 2009.

Figure 10

Cash Trigger Test (for January 2010)

Chart courtesy of Barchart.com

In Figure 10, SPY is trending above its 200-day SMA on the last trading day of December, 2009. Our Regime-O-Meter tells us we are in a "risk-on" environment. So going into January of 2010, we will hold our risk assets -- in this case, Home Depot.

Figure 11
Cash Trigger Test (for February 2010)

In Figure 11, SPY is trending above its 200-day SMA on the last trading day of January, 2010. So going into February, the market regime is "risk-on." We will hold our risk assets (Home Depot).

Figure 12
Cash Trigger Test (for March 2010)

In Figure 12, SPY is continuing to trend above its 200-day SMA on the last trading day of February, 2010. So going into March, we will continue to hold our risk assets.

Figure 13

Cash Trigger Test (for April 2010)

In Figure 13, SPY is continuing to trend above its 200-day SMA on the last trading day of March. We remain "risk-on" going into April; continue to hold Home Depot.

Figure 14

Cash Trigger Test (for May 2010)

In Figure 14, SPY is continuing to trend above its 200-day SMA on the last trading day of the month, April 30, 2010. So going into May, you guessed it, we continue to hold Home Depot.

Figure 15

Cash Trigger Test (for June 2010)

Chart courtesy of Barchart.com

In Figure 15, we've got alarms going off. SPY is trending *below* its 200-day SMA on the last trading day of May, 2010. According to our Regime-O-Meter, we are now in a "risk-off" environment. That means we'll be selling our risk asset, Home Depot. And replacing it with... what? Time to do the relative strength test on our 4 bond funds.

Figure 16

Bond Relative Strength Test (for June 2010)

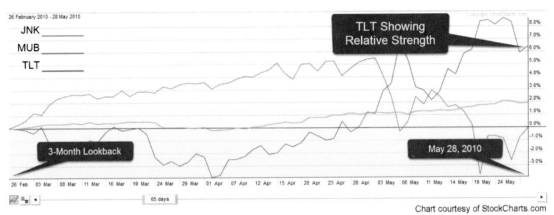

Chart courtesy of StockCharts.com

The first question is, what happened to our money market fund VMFXX? Our chart service didn't recognize the fund, so we left that out of our charting. In its place, we'll simply use the "zero" line. If all of the remaining 3 bond funds were trending below the zero line, that would be our cue to go to cash, or simply leave our money in our broker's default money market fund.

Speaking of chart services. For the Cash Trigger tests (applying our Regime-O-Meter), we've been using the free charting services at Barchart.com, specifically their "Technical Chart."

For the Relative Strength tests, however, we're going to switch to the free charting services at StockCharts.com, specifically their "PerfCharts." Comparison charts are extremely easy to construct in PerfCharts, and for the benefit of this book, the colors are a bit more vivid.

Keep in mind, though, that the charting program that comes bundled with any online broker will likely have the capability for simple comparison charts. So, make it easy on yourself.

Now, back to Figure 16. Our bond relative strength test showed the long-term bond fund TLT as the outperformer for a 3-month lookback as of May 28, 2010. That will be our pick going into June. We'll sell Home Depot and buy TLT on May 28, 2010.

What happens in a month? Come June 30, we'll go back to our Cash Trigger test and see how the broader market is holding up. Let's have a look.

Figure 17

Cash Trigger Test (for July 2010)

Chart courtesy of Barchart.com

Not good. In Figure 17, we see that SPY is continuing to trend *below* its 200-day SMA on the last trading day of June, 2010. As per our Regime-O-Meter, we remain in a "risk-off" environment going into July.

Question is, does our bond holding change? To find out, we'll do another relative strength test on our bond funds.

Figure 18

Bond Relative Strength Test (for July 2010)

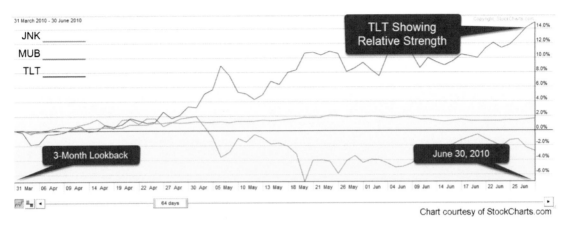

TLT remains the relative outperformer at the end of June. So, heading into July, we'll be holding our TLT. Let's see what's in store for August. First, we'll find out what our Regime-O-Meter has to say.

Figure 19

Cash Trigger Test (for August 2010)

In Figure 19, we see that SPY is continuing to trend *below* its 200-day SMA on the last trading day of July, 2010. We remain in a "risk-off" environment going into

August. Does our bond holding change? To find out, we'll do another relative strength test on our bond funds.

Figure 20

Bond Relative Strength Test (for August 2010)

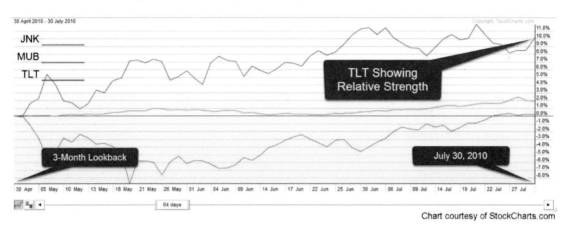

Chart courtesy of StockCharts.com

TLT remains the relative outperformer at the end of July. So, heading into August, we'll be making no changes. Let's see what's in store for September. First, we'll find out what our Regime-O-Meter has to say.

Figure 21

Cash Trigger Test (for September 2010)

Chart courtesy of Barchart.com

In Figure 21, SPY continues trending *below* its 200-day SMA. It's "risk-off" going into September. Let's do our relative strength test on our bond funds.

Figure 22

Bond Relative Strength Test (for September 2010)

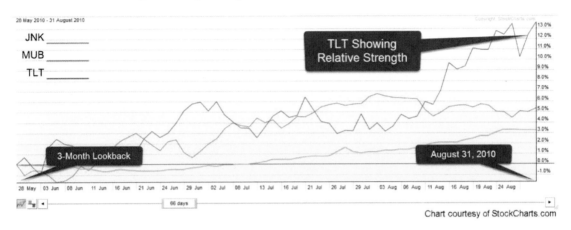

TLT remains the relative outperformer. So, heading into September, we'll be making no changes. Let's see what's in store for October. To the Regime-O-Meter.

Figure 23

Cash Trigger Test (for October 2010)

In Figure 23, SPY has broken above its 200-day SMA. We've now got a regime switch, to a "risk-on" environment going into October. On this date (September 30, 2010), we'll be selling our TLT and buying back Home Depot.

Now, I took the liberty of peeking at the remaining months of 2010, and the "risk-on" regime remains intact. In the interest of combating chart overload, let's summarize the balance of the year by simply noting that we would hold our risk asset (Home Depot) into 2011.

In summary, the year 2010 began in a "risk-on" macro environment, prompting us to hold our risk asset of Home Depot against this backdrop. A change in market regime to "risk-off" was noted for 4 months beginning in June. During this time, in place of Home Depot, we held TLT, the outperforming bond fund from our relative strength testing. The broader market returned to a "risk-on" environment beginning with October, and we swapped TLT for Home Depot for that month and the balance of the year.

Here's what it looked like in graphic form.

Figure 24

Home Depot with the Cash Trigger (2010)

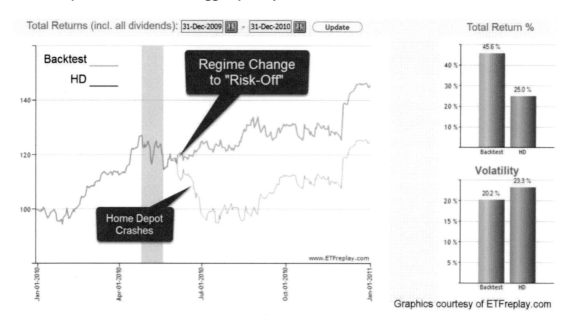

Graphics courtesy of ETFreplay.com

In Figure 24, you can see that, for the first 5 months of the year, both Home Depot (the BLUE line) and the Backtest (our Cash Trigger strategy represented by the GOLD line) were tracking together. Where they split marked the first regime switch; the bond fund TLT edged the strategy higher over the next four months while Home Depot initially plunged and then traded in a tight range until September.

When the year was up, the buy and hold investor would have seen a total return of 25.0%. Quite good by any standards. But the investor employing the Cash Trigger would have seen a total return of 45.6%.

The trade off: the Cash Trigger investor would have to spend a few minutes each month looking over stock charts. And in the case of 2010, would have made 4 trades (sell HD and buy TLT, sell TLT and buy HD), whereas the buy-and-hold investor would have made zero trades.

It worked out well for our strategy in 2010. Does it always? No. In fact, had we profiled the very next year, 2011, we would have come to a very different conclusion. Here's a graphic snapshot of Home Depot in 2011.

Figure 25

Home Depot with the Cash Trigger (2011)

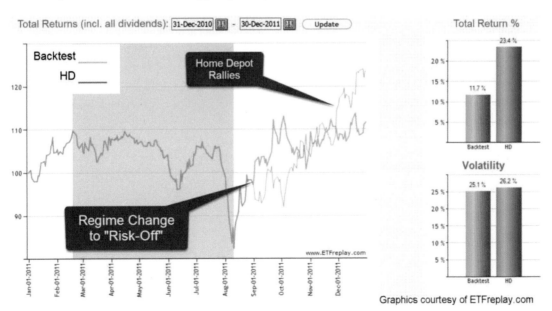

Graphics courtesy of ETFreplay.com

In Figure 25, you can see that we had a regime switch to "risk-off" beginning the month of September and lasting for the balance of the year. Home Depot and our bond selection initially diverged, but Home Depot staged an impressive rally in the next few months -- in spite of troubles in the broader market.

In the end, the buy and hold investor would have seen a total return of 23.4%. And the investor employing Cash Trigger? He would have gotten half that amount, 11.7%. To make matters worse, the Cash Trigger investor wasn't helped by an improvement in volatility (it was about the same as simply holding the stock). And max drawdown was -24.9% for both strategies, as the big drawdown for 2011 happened before the regime shift, hurting both investors.

Moral of the story: the Cash Trigger is not a short term strategy. Depending on the asset you're playing, on any given year, you may or may not come out ahead. But looking back over 17 years of data, with the individual stocks and ETFs we profiled, the winning years -- and the size of those wins -- more than made up for the periodic losses.

Chapter 6 - Trigger At Work: Case Studies

In this chapter, let's take a 10-year, behind-the-curtain look at a few individual stocks and ETFs, and see the various metrics at play when implementing the Stock Market Cash Trigger. Ten years, so we don't overwhelm with data, yet still capturing the Great Recession and a few corrections since.

Stats on Select Individual Stocks

Remember, our Stock Market Cash Trigger has us invested in equities or equity funds during "risk-on" market regimes, and out of equities (and into a bond fund) during times of "risk-off" market regimes.

But for this behind-the-curtain look, we note some of the strategies mentioned earlier (failed as they were) in order to show a comparison of data.

***

Microsoft Corporation

Figure 26

Microsoft (MSFT)

MSFT (2007-2016)	CAGR	Sharpe Ratio	MSFT Correlation	Volatility	Max Drawdown
Buy and Hold	+10.2%	0.41	1.00	28.3%	-57.9%
200-Day SMA	+4.3%	0.21	+0.68	19.2%	-38.3%
50/200-Day Cross	+3.1%	0.21	+0.68	19.2%	-36.8%
Trigger using Cash*	+13.3%	0.63	+0.69	19.4%	-20.0%
Trigger using Bonds	+18.7%	0.82	+0.53	21.3%	-20.0%

* Cash = Money Market Fund

As this is the first time we've looked at summary statistics, there are a few terms that might need explaining.

<u>CAGR</u>, or the Compound Annual Growth Rate, is the mean annual growth rate of an investment over a specified period of time longer than one year. It dampens the effect of volatility, and imagines the rate at which an investment would have grown if growth had been steady.

<u>Sharpe Ratio</u> is a formula for examining the performance of an investment or strategy by adjusting for its risk. For those into mathematics, subtract the risk-free rate (most commonly, the 90-day Treasury bill rate) from the mean return, and divide that figure by the standard deviation for the period.

If all that makes your head hurt, as it does mine, here's the thing to remember: when comparing the performance of two or more investments or strategies, the one with a higher Sharpe ratio provides a better return for the same risk.

<u>Correlation</u> measures the statistical relationship between an investment or strategy and the selected benchmark, in this case Microsoft (MSFT). In this case, using Microsoft as the benchmark allows us to see what the stock would have done as a buy and hold. A correlation of 1.0 means that the investment or strategy in question moves in virtual lockstep with the benchmark. A correlation of 0.0 means an investment or strategy has zero relationship with the benchmark, and price movements in one are unaffected by the other.

<u>Volatility</u> refers to the amount of uncertainty about the size of changes in a security's value. The higher the volatility number, the more dramatically the price of a security can fluctuate over the short term -- either up or down. A lower volatility number indicates a security's price is more apt to change at a steadier pace over time.

<u>Max Drawdown</u> is an indicator of downside risk over a specified time period. It measures the largest single drop from a peak to a trough in a portfolio -- before a new peak is achieved. In practical terms, it paints a worst case scenario for the investor. Maximum drawdown demonstrates how much would have been lost if an investment or strategy had been bought at its peak value, ridden all the way down, and sold at the low.

If an investment had never lost a dime, the max drawdown would be zero. If an investment lost everything, the max drawdown would be 100%.

While max drawdown is a backward-looking (historical) statistic, investors are well advised to factor it in when considering how much pain an investment has caused in the past.

Still with Microsoft, let's take a graphical snapshot of our earliest failed strategy, the one that tried to trade around the 200-day SMA of the stock itself.

Figure 27 shows the 10-year results for Microsoft (**BLUE** trendline and bar chart) and failed strategy (GOLD trendline and bar chart). The latter is labeled "Backtest" on the chart.

Figure 27

Microsoft: Trading the 200-Day SMA of Microsoft (2007-2016)

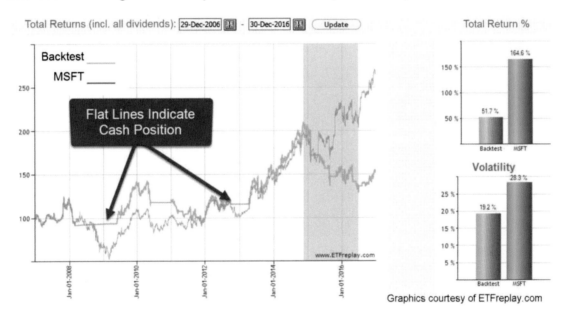

Graphics courtesy of ETFreplay.com

In Figure 27, you can easily see where the strategy went to cash a few times as Microsoft dipped below its 200-day moving average. That was certainly beneficial in 2008 and 2012 (see arrows). But in 2015, most notably, the strategy succumbed to a couple of head fakes, sitting in cash while the stock roared higher.

Here's the breakdown by years:

Figure 28
Microsoft: Trading the 200-Day SMA *of Microsoft* (2007-2016)
Annual Performance

Year	Strategy Return	MSFT Return	+ / -	Strategy Max Drawdown	MSFT Max Drawdown
2007	+19.5%	+20.8%	-1.3%	-14.1%	-14.1%
2008	-21.9%	-44.4%	+22.5%	-23.3%	-49.9%
2009	+47.8%	+60.5%	-12.7%	-9.6%	-26.5%
2010	-14.6%	-6.5%	-8.0%	-20.0%	-26.4%
2011	-15.9%	-4.5%	-11.4%	-23.9%	-16.9%
2012	+16.9%	+5.8%	+11.1%	-12.8%	-18.0%
2013	+33.6%	+44.3%	-10.7%	-13.5%	-13.5%
2014	+27.5%	+27.5%	+0.0%	-10.1%	-10.1%
2015	-20.9%	+22.7%	-43.6%	-32.3%	-16.6%
2016	-2.9%	+15.1%	-18.0%	-19.3%	-13.6%

One glance at Figure 28, specifically the + / - column, and you can see the problem. Two winning years, one neutral (no crossover of the 200-day SMA), and seven years underperforming a simple buy-and-hold strategy.

We'll skip a detailed look at the 50/200-day SMA crossover strategy, as it actually performed worse than this. Instead, let's jump to the Cash Trigger *deploying cash only* in times of "risk-off" market sentiment.

Figure 29
Microsoft: Trading the Cash Trigger *with Cash Only* (2007-2016)

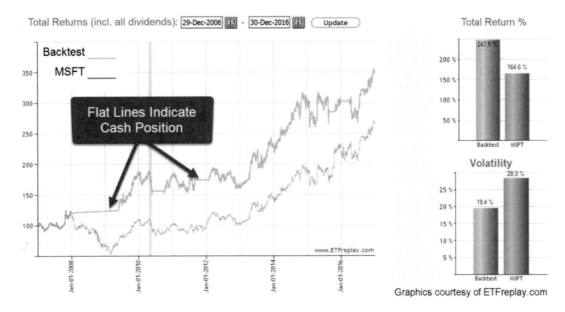

Graphics courtesy of ETFreplay.com

Remember, when we trade using the Cash Trigger, we're basing the buy/sell decisions for our equity (in this case, Microsoft) on whether SPY is above or below its 200-day SMA at the end of the month. In Figure 29, we can see that this produces a dramatic improvement in results. That "Total Return" of 247.5%, by the way, translates into the CAGR of 13.3% as noted in Figure 26.

Let's see the breakdown by years:

Figure 30

Microsoft: Trading the Cash Trigger *with Cash Only* (2007-2016)
Annual Performance

Year	Strategy Return	MSFT Return	+ / -	Strategy Max Drawdown	MSFT Max Drawdown
2007	+20.8%	+20.8%	+0.0 %	-14.1%	-14.1%
2008	+2.5%	-44.4%	+46.9%	-+0.0%	-49.9%
2009	+47.8%	+60.5%	-12.7%	-9.6%	-26.5%
2010	-2.0%	-6.5%	+4.5 %	-20.0%	-26.4%
2011	-2.9%	-4.5%	+1.6 %	-16.9%	-16.9%
2012	-7.0%	+5.8%	-12.8 %	-18.0%	-18.0%
2013	+44.3%	+44.3%	+0.0%	-13.5%	-13.5%
2014	+27.5%	+27.5%	+0.0%	-10.1%	-10.1%
2015	+1.4%	+22.7%	-21.3%	-16.6%	-16.6%
2016	+14.9%	+15.1%	-0.2%	-13.6%	-13.6%

Looking at Figure 30, we lost the edge we previously had in 2012, but more than made up for it with green in additional years, including a significant outperformance in 2008.

Let's see what it looks like when we engage the Cash Trigger *with bond rotation* in times of "risk-off" market sentiment.

Figure 31
Microsoft: Trading the Cash Trigger *with Rotating Bonds* (2007-2016)

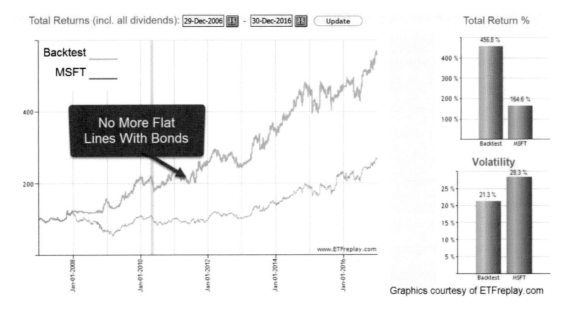

Graphics courtesy of ETFreplay.com

In Figure 31, it's easy to see the impact of trading (this equity, at least) using the Cash Trigger with a rotating bond strategy. That "Total Return" of 456.8%, by the way, translates into the CAGR of 18.7% as noted in Figure 26.

Let's see the breakdown by years:

Figure 32

Microsoft: Trading the Cash Trigger *with Rotating Bonds* **(2007-2016)**
Annual Performance

Year	Strategy Return	MSFT Return	+ / -	Strategy Max Drawdown	MSFT Max Drawdown
2007	+20.8%	+20.8%	+0.0 %	-14.1%	-14.1%
2008	+27.5%	-44.4%	+71.9%	-7.0%	-49.9%
2009	+38.5%	+60.5%	-22.0%	-15.6%	-26.5%
2010	+8.5%	-6.5%	+15.0%	-20.0%	-26.4%
2011	+11.5%	-4.5%	+16.0%	-16.9%	-16.9%
2012	-4.5%	+5.8%	-10.3%	-18.0%	-18.0%
2013	+44.3%	+44.3%	+0.0%	-13.5%	-13.5%
2014	+27.5%	+27.5%	+0.0%	-10.1%	-10.1%
2015	+3.0%	+22.7%	-19.7%	-16.6%	-16.6%
2016	+19.1%	+15.1%	+4.1%	-13.6%	-13.6%

The takeaway in Figure 32 is that not every year is a win, even with our Cash Trigger strategy with bonds. But we now have enough wins, and *significant* enough wins, that with the help of the compounding effect (generating earnings from previous earnings), we've been able to increase the CAGR from 10.2% (buy and hold) to 18.7% over 10 years.

***

Procter & Gamble Co.

Next, let's go outside our samples box and have a look at consumer products giant Procter & Gamble.

Figure 33

Procter & Gamble (PG)

PG (2007-2016)	CAGR	Sharpe Ratio	PG Correlation	Volatility	Max Drawdown
Buy and Hold	+5.8%	0.29	1.00	17.8%	-39.0%
200-Day SMA	-0.2%	negative	+0.75	13.4%	-29.4%
50/200-Day Cross	+4.8%	0.35	+0.80	14.2%	-21.0%
Trigger using Cash*	+8.1%	0.52	+0.70	12.4%	-25.0%
Trigger using Bonds	+13.3%	0.77	+0.44	15.1%	-25.1%

* Cash = Money Market Fund

Above, we see the stats for the 5 strategies. Next, let's see how trading the 200-day moving average of P&G itself looked over a 10-year period (the GOLD line, marked Backtest), relative to a buy-and-hold position (the BLUE line).

Figure 34

Procter & Gamble: Trading the 200-Day SMA of PG (2007-2016)

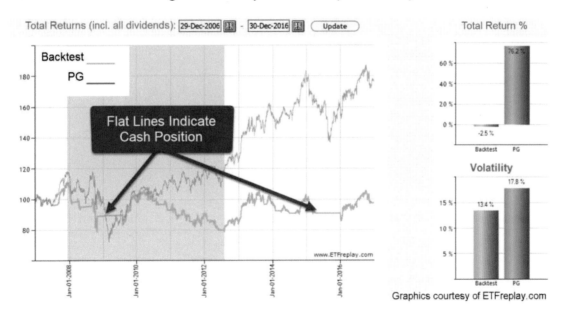

Graphics courtesy of ETFreplay.com

Procter & Gamble did not play nice with this strategy. It's hard to tell, what with the gold column on the bar chart so flat, but that's a negative -2.5% total return for the strategy over ten years. That works out to the -0.2% CAGR noted in our statistics table.

What's also hard to see, because of the size of the chart, are the numerous flat lines (cash positions) between the two arrows. In the years 2010 through 2012, for example, there were 7 times the strategy went to cash; 5 of those for only a single month. And each time was a head fake with P&G initially plunging through its 200-day SMA only to reverse course and power higher within days or weeks.

Not even swapping bonds for cash could save this strategy -- the underperformance vs. buy-and-hold remains shocking. P&G is simply a poster child of the failure of trading around a stock's own 200-day SMA.

Let's jump to a chart showing the results from employing our Cash Trigger *with bond rotation*.

Figure 35
PG: Trading the Cash Trigger *with Rotating Bonds* (2007-2016)

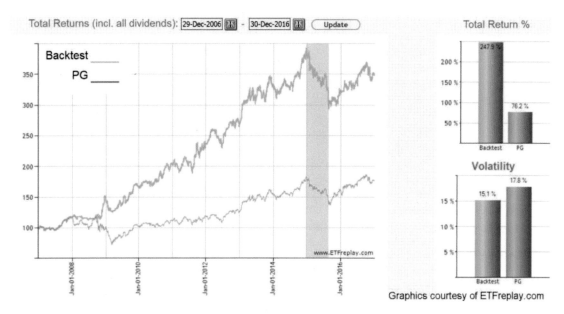

Graphics courtesy of ETFreplay.com

That looks much better. Let's see the performance year-by-year.

Figure 36

PG: Trading the Cash Trigger *with Rotating Bonds* (2007-2016)
Annual Performance

Year	Strategy Return	PG Return	+ / -	Strategy Max Drawdown	PG Max Drawdown
2007	+16.6%	+16.6%	+0.0 %	-7.4%	-7.4%
2008	+27.5%	-13.8%	+41.3%	-7.0%	-21.0%
2009	+11.5%	+1.2%	+10.3 %	-15.6%	-29.2%
2010	+22.4%	+9.4%	+13.0 %	-6.4%	-7.3%
2011	+16.4%	+7.0%	+9.4 %	-12.6%	-12.6%
2012	+13.4%	+5.2%	+8.2%	-12.0%	-12.0%
2013	+23.7%	+23.7%	+0.0%	-8.1%	-8.1%
2014	+15.4%	+15.4%	+0.0%	-6.3%	-6.3%
2015	-16.2%	-10.0%	-6.2%	-24.1%	-24.5%
2016	+8.6 %	+9.4%	-0.8%	-8.3%	-8.3%

Glancing at Figure 36, specifically the + / - column, it looks like the strategy outperformed the buy-and-hold investor in 8 years out of 10. The worst year, 2015, shows a CAGR of -16.2% and a large drawdown of -24.1%.

That massive slide was P&G tanking in spite of fact that the S&P 500 was basically flat for the year. The Cash Trigger strategy couldn't help in this situation; following the stock down into the trough.

Luckily, prior years of significant outperformance, coupled with the compounding effect, led to a good outcome for the strategy when trading P&G.

***

General Electric Company

Lest we get cocky and now think that we can blunder into the marketplace with fistfuls of cash and not pay attention to what we're doing, let's take a closer look at an old-line blue-chip name wherein our Cash Trigger strategy failed us -- maybe not in the long run, but certainly in the short.

Figure 37

General Electric (GE)

GE (2007-2017)	CAGR	Sharpe Ratio	GE Correlation	Volatility	Max Drawdown
Buy and Hold	-3.3%	0.02	1.00	30.7%	-82.7%
200-Day SMA	+4.2%	0.29	+0.52	16.0%	-27.1%
50/200-Day Cross	+3.4%	0.23	+0.55	16.9%	-30.3%
Trigger using Cash*	+2.2%	0.11	+0.61	18.7%	-45.1%
Trigger using Bonds	+6.7%	0.33	+0.45	20.4%	-44.8%

* Cash = Money Market Fund

Quick note: we're adding 2017 in this one example because there is a huge point to be made involving that year.

In the case of General Electric, buying and holding the stock for this 11-year period would have been a losing proposition. While employing the Cash Trigger improved the CAGR, it wasn't all smooth sailing; volatility was high and max drawdown a stomach-churning -44%.

But there's a larger point to be made. Let's drill down.

Figure 38

GE: Trading the Cash Trigger *with Rotating Bonds* (2007-2017)

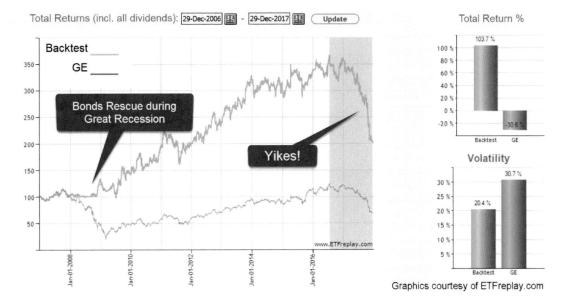

That "Yikes!" moment (Figure 38) actually lasted an entire year. In 2017, holders of the stock were down -42.9%. And so were investors who traded GE using the Cash Trigger strategy. Why didn't the strategy protect them? Because the strategy is focused on the S&P 500 index. It only goes to cash (or bonds) when SPY is trending below its 200-day moving average. In 2017, the S&P 500 was doing just fine, thank you, and the Cash Trigger never kicked in. That left the strategy to fall in lockstep with the stock.

Conversely, here's what investors trading GE *around its own* 200-day SMA got for their money.

Figure 39

GE: Trading the 200-Day SMA of GE (2007-2017)

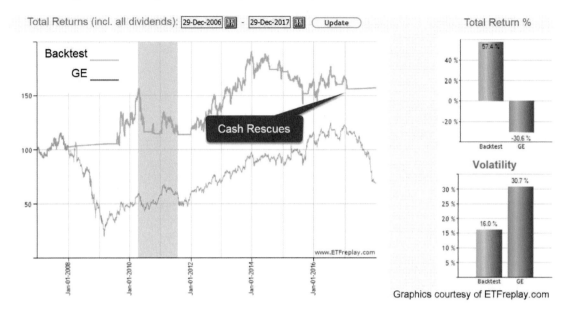

Graphics courtesy of ETFreplay.com

Investors employing the 200-Day SMA with GE went to cash on January 31, 2017 and stayed there the rest of the year, thereby avoiding GE's massive drop. They also shrank their max drawdown from -44% to -27% and reduced volatility to boot.

Of course, over the course of the entire 11 years, they underperformed Cash Trigger investors. *Dramatically* underperformed. But not in the year 2017.

While I'm not advocating the use of a stock's own 200-day SMA as a trading strategy (we've shown it to have an abysmal track record most of the time), the 200-day SMA of GE heading into 2017 was certainly signaling that something was up with the company.

Before we leave GE, let's have a look at the 11-year stats.

Figure 40

GE: Trading the Cash Trigger *with Rotating Bonds* (2007-2016)

Annual Performance

Year	Strategy Return	GE Return	+ / -	Strategy Max Drawdown	GE Max Drawdown
2007	+2.7%	+2.7%	+0.0%	-13.9%	-13.9%
2008	+27.5%	-54.0%	+81.5%	-7.0%	-65.8%
2009	+7.7%	-1.7%	+9.4%	-24.7%	-59.8%
2010	+36.6%	+24.3%	+12.3%	-18.2%	-28.4%
2011	+3.9%	+1.3%	+2.6%	-28.8%	-30.1%
2012	+19.1%	+21.2%	-2.1%	-13.5%	-13.5%
2013	+37.9%	37.9%	+0.0%	-10.2%	-10.2%
2014	-6.7%	-6.7%	+0.0%	-13.1%	-13.1%
2015	+10.2%	+27.5%	-17.3%	-17.7%	-17.7%
2016	+5.5%	+4.6%	+0.9%	-13.5%	-13.5%
2017	-42.9%	-42.9%	+0.0%	-43.5%	-43.5%

The moral of this story? The Stock Market Cash Trigger will not save you from bad stocks. In early 2017, any number of warning signs were shouting that GE was in trouble (might want to revisit Chapter 1?). Savvy investors were alert to those signals, and got out -- irrespective of what the overall market was doing.

***

Stats on Select ETFs

Let's take a closer look at a couple of ETFs. At the top of the list for the most popular ETFs, by highest average volume and according to ETF Database (ETFdb.com), there is SPY, EEM and XLF. Let's start with the latter two, and throw in a utilities sector ETF for good measure.

***

Emerging Markets ETF

Figure 41
iShares MSCI Emerging Markets ETF (EEM)

EEM (2007-2016)	CAGR	Sharpe Ratio	EEM Correlation	Volatility	Max Drawdown
Buy and Hold	+1.1%	0.17	1.00	33.5%	-66.4%
200-Day SMA	+1.9%	0.15	+0.57	19.1%	-40.3%
50/200-Day Cross	-0.1%	0.06	+0.60	20.1%	-41.1%
Trigger using Cash*	+2.7%	0.13	+0.60	20.2%	-36.6%
Trigger using Bonds	+7.7%	0.35	+0.42	22.0%	-30.7%

* Cash = Money Market Fund

Let's jump to a chart showing the results from employing our Cash Trigger *with bond rotation*, followed by the annual performance breakdown for our 10-year period.

Figure 42
EEM: Trading the Cash Trigger *with Rotating Bonds* (2007-2016)

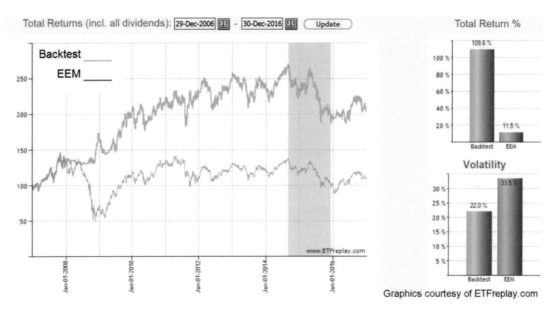

Figure 43

EEM: Trading the Cash Trigger *with Rotating Bonds* (2007-2016)
Annual Performance

Year	Strategy Return	EEM Return	+ / -	Strategy Max Drawdown	EEM Max Drawdown
2007	+33.3%	+33.3%	+0.0%	-17.7%	-17.7%
2008	+27.5%	-48.9%	+76.4%	-7.0%	-64.3%
2009	+19.3%	+68.9%	-49.6%	-15.6%	-26.4%
2010	+9.1%	+16.5%	-7.4%	-17.8%	-17.8%
2011	+4.1%	-18.8 %	+22.9%	-21.5%	-30.9%
2012	+10.2%	+19.1%	-8.9%	-18.0%	-18.0%
2013	-3.7%	-3.7%	+0.0%	-19.0%	-19.0%
2014	-3.9%	-3.9%	+0.0%	-17.7%	-17.7%
2015	-17.4%	-16.2%	-1.2%	-29.0%	-28.4%
2016	+8.1%	+10.9%	-2.8%	-10.2%	-12.2%

Our red table, Figure 43, gives up the secret: our Cash Trigger with bonds beat a buy-and-hold strategy because of massive outperformance in only 2 of 10 years. Remove 2008 and 2011 from the mix, and buy-and-hold wins. But, of course, we can't pretend the Great Recession and the broad market correction of 2011 didn't happen. They did, and our Cash Trigger with bonds strategy protected investors.

***

U.S. Financial Sector ETF

Figure 44

SPDR Financial Select Sector ETF (XLF)

XLF (2007-2016)	CAGR	Sharpe Ratio	XLF Correlation	Volatility	Max Drawdown
Buy and Hold	-0.4 %	0.14	1.00	36.0%	-82.7%
200-Day SMA	+9.6%	0.64	+0.41	14.7%	-20.5%
50/200-Day Cross	+7.9%	0.51	+0.43	15.6%	-26.2%
Trigger using Cash*	+8.1%	0.40	+0.49	17.8%	-29.8%
Trigger using Bonds	+13.3%	0.62	+0.31	19.7%	-29.8%

* Cash = Money Market Fund

Let's jump to a chart showing the results from employing our Cash Trigger *with bond rotation*, followed by the annual performance breakdown for our 10-year period.

Figure 45

XLF: Trading the Cash Trigger *with Rotating Bonds* (2007-2016)

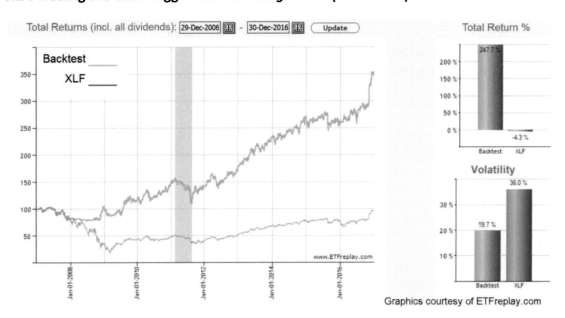

Graphics courtesy of ETFreplay.com

Figure 46

XLF: Trading the Cash Trigger *with Rotating Bonds* (2007-2016)
Annual Performance

Year	Strategy Return	XLF Return	+ / -	Strategy Max Drawdown	XLF Max Drawdown
2007	-19.2%	-19.2%	+0.0%	-24.6%	-24.6%
2008	+27.5%	-55.0%	+82.5%	-7.0%	-67.6%
2009	+12.0%	+17.6%	-5.6%	-15.6%	-51.2%
2010	+26.3%	+11.9%	+14.4%	-16.5%	-21.0%
2011	-3.1%	-17.1%	+14.0%	-29.8%	-33.7%
2012	+21.9%	+28.4%	-6.5%	-16.4%	-16.4%
2013	+35.5%	35.5%	+0.0%	-6.9%	-6.9%
2014	+15.1%	+15.1%	+0.0%	-7.3%	-7.3%
2015	-3.4%	-1.7%	-1.7%	-12.7%	-12.7%
2016	+34.0%	+22.6%	+11.4%	-9.6%	-17.5%

I hate to keep coming back to the year 2008, and yet I do. The financial sector was particularly hard hit that year, with the sector ETF cut in half and buy-and-hold investors suffering through a drawdown of more than -67%. The Cash Trigger with the bond boost? Not so bad. A -7% drawdown and an actual positive return of +27.5% for the year.

***

U.S. Utility Sector ETF

Figure 47

SPDR Utilities Select Sector ETF (XLU)

XLU (2007-2016)	CAGR	Sharpe Ratio	XLU Correlation	Volatility	Max Drawdown
Buy and Hold	+6.8%	0.40	1.00	18.9%	-46.5%
200-Day SMA	+6.5%	0.48	+0.69	13.1%	-17.6%
50/200-Day Cross	+6.7%	0.49	+0.71	13.4%	-21.6%
Trigger using Cash*	+7.9%	0.50	+0.67	12.7%	-17.6%
Trigger using Bonds	+13.1%	0.76	+0.42	15.3%	-17.4%

* Cash = Money Market Fund

I wanted to include a representative sample of utility stocks since they have developed a reputation as a quasi safe haven in the face of broader market turmoil. The utility sector ETF XLU seems a logical target. And it looks like the Cash Trigger with *bond rotation* beat it handily for the 10-year period, and offered a considerably smaller max drawdown as a bonus.

Let's jump to a chart showing the results from employing our Cash Trigger *with bond rotation*, followed by the annual performance breakdown for our 10-year period.

Figure 48

XLU: Trading the Cash Trigger *with Rotating Bonds* (2007-2016)

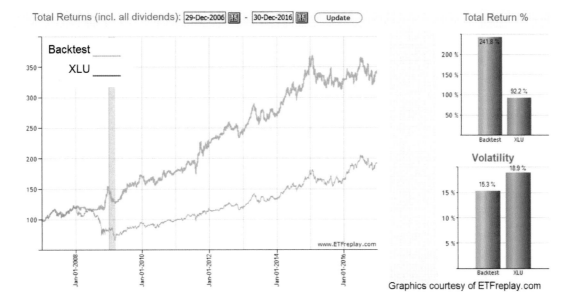

Graphics courtesy of ETFreplay.com

Figure 49

XLU: Trading the Cash Trigger *with Rotating Bonds* (2007-2016)

Annual Performance

Year	Strategy Return	XLU Return	+ / -	Strategy Max Drawdown	XLU Max Drawdown
2007	+18.4%	+18.4%	+0.0%	-11.7%	-11.7%
2008	+27.5%	-28.9%	+56.4%	-7.0%	-39.7%
2009	+12.6%	11.7%	+0.9%	-15.6%	-24.5%
2010	+4.7%	+5.3%	-0.6%	-9.0%	-9.4%
2011	+26.7%	19.6%	+7.1%	-11.3%	-11.3%
2012	+7.6%	+1.0%	+6.6%	-9.9%	-9.9%
2013	+13.0%	13.0%	+0.0%	-12.0%	-12.0%
2014	+28.7%	28.7%	+0.0%	-9.2%	-9.2%
2015	-7.2%	-4.9%	-2.3%	-15.2%	-15.7%
2016	+4.3%	+16.1%	-11.8%	-12.4%	-12.4%

Looking at our red table (Figure 49), the takeaway for me is that utilities may have shown a certain relative strength over equities during the Great Recession (2008), "only" generating a loss of -28.9% in the face of the S&P's -36.8% haircut, but bonds ruled. Specifically the TLT long-term bond fund, in which the Cash Trigger investors spent much of that year invested.

***

U.S. Large and Mid Cap Stocks (S&P 500 Index) ETF

Our Cash Trigger strategy revolves around SPY (and its relationship to its 200-day SMA), so why not splay out the nitty-gritty on this fund? Let's do it.

Figure 50

SPDR S&P 500 ETF (SPY)

SPY (2007-2016)	CAGR	Sharpe Ratio	SPY Correlation	Volatility	Max Drawdown
Buy and Hold	+6.9%	0.38	1.00	20.8%	-55.2%
200-Day SMA	+10.1%	0.76	+0.60	12.5%	-17.3%
50/200-Day Cross	+8.6%	0.64	+0.62	12.8%	-17.5%
Trigger using Cash*	+9.6%	0.62	+0.60	12.5%	-17.3%
Trigger using Bonds	+14.9%	0.85	+0.29	15.2%	-17.4%

* Cash = Money Market Fund

Let's jump first to a chart showing the results from employing our Cash Trigger *using cash only* during times of "risk-off" market sentiment.

I wanted to include this (see Figure 51) simply because it makes it visually easy to identify both the Crash of 2008 (first arrow), as well as a number of other corrections along the way, including the correction of 2011 (second arrow) which began in late April and ran through September, leading to a 20% drawdown in the S&P 500 index.

And because SPY tracks the market leading indicator on which the Cash Trigger strategy is based, the mechanics of strategy are perhaps most evident in this chart.

Figure 51
SPY: Trading the Cash Trigger *with Cash Only* (2007-2016)

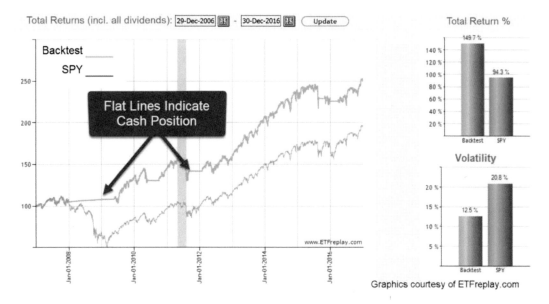

And next, the results from employing our Cash Trigger *with bond rotation*.

Figure 52
SPY: Trading the Cash Trigger *with Rotating Bonds* (2007-2016)

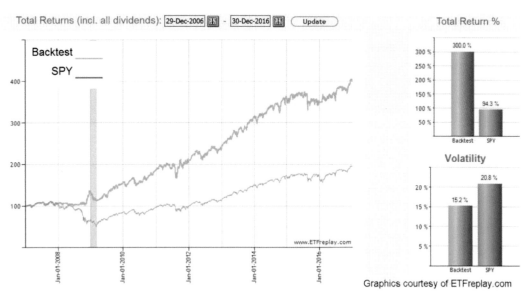

And finally, the annual performance breakdown for our 10-year period.

Figure 53

SPY: Trading the Cash Trigger *with Rotating Bonds* (2007-2016)
Annual Performance

Year	Strategy Return	SPY Return	+ / -	Strategy Max Drawdown	SPY Max Drawdown
2007	+5.1%	+5.1%	+0.0%	-9.9%	-9.0%
2008	+27.5%	-36.8%	+64.3%	-7.0%	-47.6%
2009	+15.0%	+26.4%	-11.4%	-15.6%	-27.1%
2010	+20.9%	+15.1%	+5.8%	-12.0%	-15.7%
2011	+12.7%	+1.9%	+10.8%	-17.3%	-18.6%
2012	+13.8%	+16.0%	-2.2%	-9.7%	-9.7%
2013	+32.3%	+32.3%	+0.0%	-5.6%	-5.6%
2014	+13.5%	+13.5%	+0.0%	-7.3%	-7.3%
2015	-2.8%	+1.3%	-4.1%	-11.9%	-11.9%
2016	+14.7%	+12.0%	+2.7%	-5.5%	-10.3%

One final note on the red tables (i.e. Figure 53). In the + / - column, you've probably noticed that some years consistently show +0.0%, regardless of the stock or ETF we're profiling. Those are the years in which the strategy never kicked in, leaving the stock or ETF to dictate returns, as well as max drawdowns.

***

Chapter 7 - Caveats and Q&A

So many market timing models are black boxes; data goes in, proprietary algorithms stir the brew, and out pops trade recommendations devoid of context. I wanted to create a model that was not only transparent, but one that made a certain intuitive, logical sense.

The 200-day moving average, when applied to the ETF equivalent of the S&P 500, is a well-established trend indicator. That other risk assets are pulled along by the gravity of that moving average is not only logical, but bears out in testing. And finally, the use of fixed income as a hedge, *but only when needed as a hedge*, allows the model to maximize gains in either regime.

The icing on the cake? A simple bond rotation technique that works to maximize returns during "risk-off" regimes.

That said, no mechanical timing model is perfect, and certainly not this one. There will be years that beat the benchmarks, and years the model will underperform. The exceptional results we achieved for the stock and fund examples we profiled are due in no small part by the extended time frame over which we conducted the backtests.

That time frame, 17 years in most of our examples, included two major market crashes and a number of smaller corrections, allowing the Cash Trigger to kick in and protect profits even as the strategy gave up some of those profits in other years.

Which leads to the first caveat...

CAVEAT #1 - THE MODEL MAY NOT WORK AS A SHORT-TERM STRATEGY. Not every year sees a significant correction, but practically every year delivers multiple threats of such a correction -- head fakes and false signals, times when the market appears to be moving in one direction only to end up reversing course and moving in the other.

The model was designed to kick into gear and protect during corrections, but in order to do so it must necessarily kick into gear during a number of *threats* of corrections, chewing up trading commissions, generating potentially taxable capital gains, and sitting out markets that end up moving higher.

In that respect, one or two or three years of underperformance should not be used as an indictment against the strategy.

CAVEAT #2 - NOT EVERY STOCK OR FUND WILL BENEFIT. We sampled a number of individual stocks, mostly large-caps identified by their top rankings within the S&P 500 index, as well as a few of the more popular ETFs. We did not test the universe of stocks and funds, nor even a large number. Presumably, there are stocks and funds to which trading the strategy would not benefit. Most notably, stocks of companies that are in trouble for reasons that have nothing to do with the broader market. So--traders beware (as always).

Questions & Answers

///

 Q   Two Books, Two Strategies. Is this the same cash trigger that you discussed in your previous book, *The 12% Solution*?

A   It is not. The cash trigger incorporated into *The 12% Solution* uses a different methodology. *The 12% Solution* is a tightly-focused model with minimal moving parts and an ever-present bond component.

What worked for *The 12% Solution* wasn't necessarily optimal for trying to protect risk assets outside of that model, from the vast array of ETFs to individual stocks. Adjustments were necessary. Hence, the Stock Market Cash Trigger.

///

Q   Why Different Bond Universes. In *The 12% Solution*, you have a bond universe of 2 funds. Here, you've got a bond universe of 4. Should those of us following *The 12% Solution* adjust our bond universe to include all 4 funds?

A   No. As odd as this may sound, when backtesting *The 12% Solution*, adding MUB and VMFXX (or any money market fund) to the bond mix actually undercut performance in that model. Conversely, the addition of those two funds contributes to returns for the Stock Market Cash Trigger.

What's going on here? The difference is that *The 12% Solution* has an ever-present bond allocation, good times and bad, while the Stock Market Cash Trigger only has bonds come into the picture during times of market stress. That, and the fact that each model uses a slightly different timing mechanism to determine market stress, accounts for the different mix of bonds required to maximize performance in each.

In short, each model is optimized for a specific purpose. *The 12% Solution* is a stand-alone conservative investment strategy that doesn't venture outside a small group of ETFs. The Stock Market Cash Trigger, on the other hand, provides the opportunity to play and protect any risk equity or ETF outside of *The Solution*.

///

Q   Monthly vs. Daily Trading. The Cash Trigger strategy checks once a month to see if SPY is trending above or below its 200-day simple moving average. But in reality, that price line could cross the moving average at any time. Why not check daily?

A   In some cases, you could improve your performance by checking -- and potentially trading -- daily vs. monthly. You'll also get whipsawed around more. Meaning, you'll be subject to many more false signals of breakouts and breakdowns, and as a result, incur more transaction costs.

I opted to go with once a month as it provided near-optimal metrics, kept trading commissions to a minimum, and didn't require me to be glued to the computer every hour of every trading day.

///

Q First Day vs. Last Day. You would have investors check the Cash Trigger strategy on the last day of the month. Why the last day of the month? Why not the first, or any other day for that matter?

A Checking the charts on the last day of the month -- and executing a trade if need be -- demonstrated a *slight* advantage over the first day of the month. That, over the 17-year backtest. That's in keeping with research that suggests a slight historical bias to the plus side for end-of-month rebalancing.

That same research, it should be noted, is showing that bias to be less evident in recent years. And as far as any other day of the month, I didn't have the tools or the patience to run the numbers on days other than the first and last. So the jury's out on whether the strategy could be tweaked to provide even further upside by switching to a different day of the month.

///

Q Simple vs. Exponential Moving Averages. When you were trading around the 50-day and the 200-day moving averages, you used simple moving averages. Have you tried exponential moving averages? If so, did they perform better?

A I didn't personally run the numbers on exponential moving averages (EMAs), relying instead on research conducted by Nate Vernon for the Hulbert Financial Digest. [EMAs place more weight on recent market activity, whereas SMAs equally weigh each day.]

In a November 11, 2013 article, Vernon concluded that his research -- going back decades -- provided no basis for believing that EMAs were any better than simple moving averages. He studied EMA strategies both with and without trading envelopes, and explored lengths ranging from 20 days to 252 days.

Said Vernon: "In no cases were the returns of these EMAs superior to those of simple moving averages, and often were worse."

///

Q Capital Gains Taxes. In your 17-year examples, your strategy is generating 60 or so trades. That's 60 more trades than buy-and-hold, and each one generating capital gains at tax time. Have you taken that into consideration?

A Each investor's tax situation will be different, so I can't presume to offer blanket advice except to say that tax implications should always be a factor in one's decision to sell equities. That said, two things to keep in mind.

If you limit equity trades to a tax-deferred or tax-free retirement account, you won't be taxed for capital gains along the way (taxes are due on withdrawals with the former, and avoided altogether with the latter).

If you must trade in a traditional (taxable) brokerage account, you should be reasonably sure your "sells" will prevent sufficient losses to offset any expected capital gains taxes. You might not know that for certain each time you pull the trigger, but as time goes on you should be able to accumulate evidence that your strategy is outpacing the tax man.

///

Q One Bond. To save on commissions, if I didn't want to switch around between bond funds, is there a single fund that that you would recommend?

A TLT will give you the most bang for the buck, but with a higher volatility and drawdown. To reduce those risk metrics, you might try AGG, the iShares Core U.S. Aggregate Bond ETF. It offers broad exposure to investment grade U.S. bonds. In my tests, when serving as the only bond option, it performed better than SHY, but not nearly as well as TLT (ignoring the heightened risks associated with TLT).

///

Q Time Frame on Chart. When you're doing the regime test once a month and looking at the 200-day moving average of SPY, what is the time frame on the chart supposed to be?

A   It doesn't really matter. The time frame on the chart won't change the moving average. Use what's comfortable. I used a 9-month chart (lookback period), for the examples in the book.

However, in the occasional instance when the price line and the moving average line converge into a tight spot, you might have to reduce the chart's time frame to a month or two in order to better see the positioning of both lines.

///

Q   One Pick. If I wanted to use this strategy on one stock, what should it be?

A   Just one? I wouldn't pick a stock. I'd pick a broad-market ETF like SPY. It would track with the strategy most accurately (it *is* the strategy, to a large extent). Or QQQ, the NASDAQ-100 index ETF, if I was willing to handle a little extra volatility in return for some extra CAGR.

///

Q   Why No Gold? Why are the rotation candidates only bond funds? Did you try gold, which has always been a classic hedge?

A   The criteria for candidates: that they contribute to a rotational strategy that improves CAGR, or lowers volatility, or reduces max drawdown, or some combination of the three. Gold failed, despite its reputation as a hedge.

///

Q   Please No. Could you please not use the word Regime-O-Meter ever again?

A   No promises.

///

Q Flash Crash. Can this strategy protect during a flash crash?

A No. A flash crash is a very rapid, deep and volatile plunge in security prices that takes place in a short period of time -- typically in minutes. As I write these words, we are just a few weeks past the biggest point drop in history for the Dow Jones Industrial Average (-1,175 points). That would be Monday, February 5, 2018. The strategy did not protect.

Why? The strategy is based on the 200-day moving average of SPY -- a stand-in for the S&P 500 index. It takes a number of days of significant trend reversal to begin to move the arc of that average toward that reversal.

In other words, the strategy works only when the marketplace telegraphs an upcoming trend reversal. In flash crashes or abrupt market selloffs, it doesn't.

///

Q Dramatic. I have to tell you, this strategy seems awfully dramatic. When the regime changes, you sell everything, *everything*. And then buy one thing, a bond fund. I think I might be stressed to make these gigantic, all-or-nothing trades.

A I hear you. Followed to a T, and depending on one's portfolio, the strategy can seem dramatic. Keep in mind, though, that doing nothing as the economy and the stock market slides into a bear market can be pretty dramatic, too.

That said, it needn't be an all-or-nothing proposition. If you're uncomfortable, you always have the option to ignore the strategy, or maybe go in partially. For example, selling some percentage of your position in a risk asset, and buying the selected bond fund with the proceeds. So, you might end up with 50% MSFT and 50% bond fund for the duration of the "risk-off "regime. Your results will vary, but some protection will still be afforded.

///

Q   Panacea. Is your strategy a panacea?

A   No.

///

Q   Be All and End All. Is your strategy the "be all and end all"?

A   No.

///

Q   Sliced Bread. Is your strategy the best thing since sliced bread?

A   Maybe.

///

Q   Last Words. Do you have any last words?

A   Regime-O-Meter.

Chapter 8 - Tools

The most useful tool you have in your possession is likely your broker's website. Check there first to see if you can construct the kind of charts you need for the Stock Market Cash Trigger -- charts capable of moving averages (look for buttons marked "studies" or "indicators" on a stock chart), as well as the ability to construct simple comparison charts for multiple securities or funds.

In the event you need to look elsewhere, consider the following services which we used in the book.

Barchart (Barchart.com)

We used the free charting services at Barchart.com when creating charts to explain moving averages and implement the Regime-O-Meter testing. Type in the stock or ETF symbol you want, and when the detail page pulls up, note the small chart on the page and click the button marked "Full Chart."

When applying our Regime-O-Meter to SPY and its 200-day SMA, we specifically used their "Technical Chart" (click link in left-hand margin) along with the following settings:

- Enter Symbol: SPY
- Chart Type: Basic
- Settings: Candlesticks
- Settings: Price Scale
- Period: Daily
- Study: Moving Average, Simple (200)

While we used a different service to conduct the relative strength tests for our 4 bond funds, we could have stayed with this service. If you plan to do so, stick with their "Technical Chart" but change a couple of things:

- Enter Symbol: TLT (you can use any of the 4 bond funds here)
- Chart Type: Comparison Chart
- Symbol 1 - JNK
- Symbol 2 - MUB
- Symbol 3 - leave blank
- Settings: Line
- Settings: % Change Scale
- Period: either 3-Months, or plug in specific 3-month calendar dates
- Study: Remove the SMA

Barchart.com did not recognize the money market fund VMFXX, so we would have left that out of our charting. In its place, we would simply use the "zero" line. If all of the remaining 3 bond funds are trending below the zero line, that's our cue to go to cash, or simply leave our money in our broker's default money market fund.

StockCharts (StockCharts.com)

We used the free charting services at Stockcharts.com to construct the charts for our relative strength tests for our 4 bond funds.

- From their home page, click "Free Charts" in the upper menu.
- Scroll to the section marked "PerfCharts." Type in the symbols for your bond funds and click "Go." Your comparison chart will fill the screen.
- Notice the slider just beneath the chart, preset to 200 days. That's the current lookback period.
- Because we use a 3-month lookback (63 trading days) for the bond test, you'll need to double-click the "200 days" and type in 64 and then enter. That will give you the 63-day *return* we need.

If you're backtesting, you can grab the slider with your mouse (I know, what's that?) and move it to the left until you get the dates you want. The dates are up in the left-hand corner of the chart. You can fine tune (i.e. creep one day at a time) by clicking the arrows at either end of the slider. Add or subtract days to the slider handle to expand or contract the time frame.

As with the previous service, StockCharts did not recognize the money market fund VMFXX, so we left that out of our charting. In its place, we simply use the "zero" line. If all of the remaining 3 bond funds are trending below the zero line, that's our cue to go to cash, or simply leave our money in our broker's default money market fund.

Additional Tools and Informational Sites

-- ETFreplay.com - subscription service providing data, analysis and backtesting.

-- ETF Database (ETFdb.com) - premier source of information on ETF investing.

A Note To The Reader

Thank You

Thank you for reading *Stock Market Cash Trigger*. I sincerely hope you found it a contribution to your investment goals.

Gaining exposure as an independent author relies mostly on word-of-mouth, so if you have the time and inclination, please consider leaving a short review on Amazon or Goodreads. Your thoughts are important and I would be honored to have you share them.

-- David Alan Carter

Sign Up for the Cash Trigger Newsletter

Newsletter: No strategy should be carved in stone. Should the markets shift and the *Cash Trigger* strategy needs adapting to keep it ahead of the game, I'll notify readers via an email newsletter.

Members Page: When you sign up, you'll receive a "Welcome" email with a link to access the *Members Page*. There, you'll find strategy updates and Q&As that have accumulated since publication. In addition, I track how one variation of the strategy -- employing only SPY during risk-on regimes -- has fared over the years since publication. View total return charts from 2008 to the most recent full year, as well as tables showing year-by-year performance and related risk metrics – all updated annually.

Sign up at the following location:

https://www.davidalancarter.com/triggersignup

About The Author

Growing up in the Southern Great Plains region, author David Alan Carter was taught from an early age to work hard and protect what you've got. The former came naturally. The latter, protecting what you've got (i.e. money), took some twists and turns throughout the years.

One particularly gut-wrenching turn: the Great Recession. "That was a watershed moment," Carter recalls. "Like so many others impacted, my attitude toward investing would be forever changed."

Cut to present. With 20 years of investing experience ranging from buy-and-hold to swing trading to high-frequency day trading, Carter has distilled those lessons learned into simple, verifiable and repeatable trading strategies that can benefit anyone interested in making money -- and keeping money -- in the stock market.

Stock Market Cash Trigger is the second in a series on investing and personal finance.

_____

Trader
Author, Publisher, former Newspaper Columnist
Bachelors in Business Management, Oklahoma State University

Also by the author...
The 12% Solution

Disclaimer

No Financial Advice

The entire contents of this book and any associated media (website, newsletter, email alert service, etc.), are provided for educational, informational, and entertainment purposes only. We (the author, editors and publishers) are not securities brokers or dealers and we are not financial advisers, analysts or planners. We are neither licensed nor qualified to provide investment advice. The information contained within this book is not an offer to buy or sell securities. Nothing within these pages or on associated media takes into account the particular investment objectives, financial situations, or needs of individuals, therefore should not be construed as a personal recommendation. WE ARE NOT SOLICITING ANY ACTION.

Do Your Own Due Diligence

The information provided is not intended as a complete source of information on any particular company, investment, asset or market. An individual should never make investment decisions based solely on information contained within our book or any associated media (or any book or website, for that matter). READERS SHOULD ASSUME THAT ALL INFORMATION PROVIDED REGARDING COMPANIES, INVESTMENTS, ASSETS OR MARKETS IS NOT TRUSTWORTHY UNLESS VERIFIED BY THEIR OWN INDEPENDENT RESEARCH.

Investing In Securities Is High Risk

Any individual who chooses to invest in any securities should do so with caution. Investing in securities is inherently speculative and carries a high degree of risk; you may lose some or all of the money that is invested, and if you engage in margin transactions your loss may exceed the amount invested. Before acting on any analysis, advice, trade triggers or recommendations, investors should consider whether the security or strategy in question is suitable for their particular circumstances and, if necessary, seek professional advice. You must decide your own suitability to trade.

YOU ASSUME ALL RISKS AND COSTS ASSOCIATED WITH ANY TRADING YOU CHOOSE TO UNDERTAKE.

Past Performance No Guarantee

Trading results can never be guaranteed. The information provided in this book and associated media regarding the past performance of any security or strategy is only representative of historical conditions in the marketplace, and is not to be construed as a guarantee that such conditions will exist in the future or that such performance will be achieved in the future. The price and value of investments referred to in this book and any associated media, and the income from them may go down as well as up, and investors may realize losses on any investments. Past performance is no guarantee of future results. Future returns are not guaranteed, and a loss of original capital may occur. ONLY INVEST WITH MONEY THAT YOU CAN AFFORD TO LOSE.

Differences in Portfolio Performance

Readers should be aware that numerous variables including timing of trade, trading commission, slippage and execution issues, may result in actual portfolio performance to differ measurably from modeled and backtested strategy performance.

Reliability Of Data

The contents of this book and any associated media -- text, graphics, links and other materials -- are based on public information that we consider reliable, but we do not represent that it is accurate or complete, and it should not be relied on as such. This book and associated media may contain inaccuracies, typographical errors and other errors. All information and materials are provided on an "as is" and "as available" basis, without warranty or condition of any kind either expressed or implied. The author does not warrant the quality, accuracy, reliability, adequacy or completeness of any of such information and material, and expressly disclaims any liability for errors or omissions in such information and material. Opinions expressed herein are the author's opinions as of the date of publication of those opinions, and may or may not be updated.

No Warranties

Stock Market Cash Trigger does not guarantee or warrant the quality, accuracy, completeness, timeliness, appropriateness or suitability of the information or of any product or services referenced. The author assumes no obligation to update the information or advise on further developments concerning topics mentioned. This book may contain links to Internet sites. Such links are provided for reference only and were independently developed by parties other than the author. We are not responsible for the contents of any such linked sites and do not assume any responsibility for the accuracy or appropriateness of the information contained at such sites. The inclusion of any link does not imply endorsement by the author of the site. Use of any such linked site is at the user's own risk.

We Will Not Be Liable

To the fullest extent of the law, we (the author, editors and publishers) will not be liable to any person or entity for the quality, accuracy, completeness, reliability, or timeliness of the information provided within this book and associated media, or for any direct, indirect, consequential, incidental, special or punitive damages whatsoever and howsoever caused, that may arise out of or in connection with the use or misuse of the information we provide. Such referenced "damages" may include, but not be limited to, lost profits, loss of opportunities, trading losses, or damages that may result from any inaccuracy or incompleteness of this information, whether such damages arise in contract, tort, strict liability, negligence, equity or statute law or by way of any other legal theory. We disclaim any liability for unauthorized use or reproduction of any portion of the information from this book or associated media.

Consent and Agreement

Please be advised that your continued use of this book or the information provided herein or with any associated media shall indicate your consent and agreement to these terms.

Made in the USA
Monee, IL
01 March 2020